THE
CLASH OF
KINGDOMS

THE
CLASH OF
KINGDOMS

Rediscovering Our
Role In Earth's
Greatest Battle

STEVE HARRISON

Ardor Media
P.O. Box 8940
Minneapolis, MN 55408

Dedication

I would like to dedicate this book to all those who have been ruined by His love and have joined His rescue mission of planet earth. Let us unite our hearts in jubilant service to our eternal King and Friend. May we honor Him and the Kingdom He so wisely rules.

For He alone is worthy!

Acknowledgments

My immediate family: Martha, Molly, and Dan for your incredible spiritual sensitivity and insight.

The editors: Jessica Gaylord, Ric Jacobsen Amanda Price, and Michelle Winger for your talented and faithful service.

Cover design: Sheryl Thornberg for your skill in conveying words into art.

Table of Contents

Part Three: The Road to Victory

FOREWORD

Let me ask you a question.

What kind of a man would use a rock for a pillow?

Well, in Jacob's case, he was a very tired and desperate man. (Gen. 28:11) He was running from his past, without strength, and yet he had the hope of the fulfillment of the blessing and a longing for his destiny.

But did you know that there was another man who rested his head on a rock? This man was John, the Beloved. He placed his head against the chest of the rock who is Jesus (John 13:23). He did it, not so much because he was tired, but because he was desperate... in a different way... desperate because of his passion for the one that loved him. As a result, both of these men experienced a wonderful glimpse into the realities of the kingdom of God.

If you are like me, and I think you are, you are becoming more and more filled with that desperation as well. We share a longing for the powerful destiny that is promised to us and demonstrated by Jesus. This is the plan of God for us... His kingdom on earth, fully and completely engaging, and overcoming, the kingdom of darkness with power.

We share a deep desire for something more than we have yet experienced. *We desire the presence of God that is so powerfully revealed that it causes even unbelievers to believe.* It is a place where the presence of the Holy Spirit moves freely bringing conviction filled with a passion for holiness... because of an increased passion for Jesus.

This is His desire for His church. A church that is so filled with His glory that the "gates of hell would not prevail against it". It is a reality that can only come from the Lord responding to desperate, broken hearts that are not satisfied with where they have been. Only longing for where He wants them to go.

This is the heart of Steve Harrison. As you read, you will find that he has written a book that seems to unfold the heart of God with the grace of conviction. It reveals the compassion of Jesus drawing us to pursue the higher revelation of His kingdom and its impact on earth.

I am convinced that as you turn each page you will also find yourself joining the author in 'laying your head on the rock'.

Together in Mission,

Mike Smith

Senior Pastor

Redeeming Love Church

Maplewood, Minnesota

Introduction

I am a product of the Jesus People Movement. In 1972, I came face to face with biblical Christianity. It did not compromise or cater to my self-serving lifestyle. It was radically relevant. Soon after, I joined a ministry called the Agape Force and moved near Keith Green, Leonard Ravenhill, Winkie Pratney, and David Wilkerson in East Texas. For sixteen years, I enjoyed the privilege of helping ministry teams and centers throughout the United States. I witnessed the transforming power of the gospel shake my generation.

During this time, God deposited a passion for revival that has never left. This passion led my family and me to move into the urban core of South Minneapolis in 1998. There, we began a ministry called Bethany Urban Development. Our focus was on rescuing heroin addicts, homeless alcoholics, and refugees trapped in false religions.

While living in this at-risk neighborhood, I became acutely aware of the spiritual darkness oppressing those trapped in the city. I became obsessed with a desire to see God's Kingdom come to the places of greatest need. As a result, we started a prayer coalition consisting of key church and ministry leaders of the area. We saw many positive results, but a prevailing darkness seemed to thwart any major breakthroughs.

Finally, in our desperation, God led our ministry to do something so simple but so profound. He said, "I do not want you to pursue prayer as an activity or an event. I want your prayers to become a lifestyle." His words led us to nightly prayer sessions that became the focus of our ministry. These prayer times led to many miracles and spiritual revelations. As a result, we began to disengage from this world's system. Our way of thinking began to change dramatically. We felt more in rhythm with God's heart than ever before. During this time, He also showed us what was coming to our land and our role in His Kingdom.

In John 16:13b, Jesus describes the ministry of the Holy Spirit: "He will tell you what is yet to come." God does not want us to be caught unawares. He knows where He is going and what is coming. However, our only safeguard from spiritual error and neglect is to live in an ongoing communion with Him—a prayer lifestyle.

King Hezekiah was a man who did "what was right in the eyes of the Lord" (2 Kings 18:3). Because of his earnest prayers, God delivered Judah from the Assyrians (see 2 Kings 19:14–37) and even delivered Hezekiah from a life-threatening disease (see 2 Kings 20:4–6).

Shortly after his illness, King Hezekiah received an official delegation from Babylon. He was more than happy to show these envoys his royal treasury, thinking Babylon possessed no threat to his kingdom. Nevertheless, the local prophet, who walked in communion with God, saw the unseen threat:

> Then Isaiah said to Hezekiah, "Hear the word of the Lord: The time will surely come when everything in your palace, and all that your predecessors have stored up until this day, will be carried off to Babylon. Nothing will be left, says the Lord" (2 Kings 20:16–17).

Tragically, Hezekiah responded to the danger with self-serving indifference. "'The word of the LORD you have spoken is good,' Hezekiah replied. For he thought, 'Will there not be peace and security in my lifetime?'" (2 Kings 20:19).

The kingdom of Babylon is still around, and I believe it poses an even graver danger to the Church. Part of its strength comes from our miscalculation of its current and future threat. In many minds, the danger is simply minimized or ignored. We have often chosen coexistence over confrontation. As a result, Babylon is carrying off our biblical values and replacing them with its own.

True Christianity places people into strategic positions. True Christians will see things others do not. They will clearly mark their boundaries, lifestyle, and values. They will demonstrate a superior way of living through their words and deeds.

The Clash of Kingdoms is the third and final installment of the *Warrior Bride Series*. The spiritual principles and insights of this book have come as God has led us into a deeper prayer lifestyle and a better understanding of our spiritual destiny. I believe these truths are critical for seeing a much-needed revival in our land.

Part One

THE BATTLE LINES ARE DRAWN

Chapter 1

✝HE RISE OF BABYLON

---

*This is still a dangerous world. It's a world of madmen
and uncertainty and potential mental losses.*
—GEORGE W. BUSH[1]

*They say to God, 'Get lost! We've no interest in you or your ways.
Why should we have dealings with God Almighty? What's there
in it for us?'*
—JOB 21:14-15 MSG

We had just dropped off our wives and children at a motel in Laredo, Texas, after a yearlong missions trip. My son-in-law, Adam, and I were returning to the border town of Nuevo Laredo to pick up the remainder of our household goods in our friend Rene's fruit truck. I was tired after driving all night from central Mexico, but we had four friends to help us load our van and trailer. All seemed normal when we pulled up to the vacant lot next to the Oxxo gas station.

As the process of loading began, a police squad car pulled up, and two officers got out. My Spanish was not good enough to understand their questions, but I assumed they were just curious about what we were doing. I continued to pack the trailer while my friends spoke with them. Surprisingly, another police vehicle came, then another, then another. I could tell it was not going well. They were now demanding money and were not taking no for an answer.

Suddenly, their aggressiveness started to take a dangerous turn. They confiscated our cell phones and searched our pockets for money. Rene resisted, and a gun barrel was quickly stuck in his gut. We were lined up spread-eagle style while their guns were drawn. Soon we discovered they were actually members of the notorious Zeta drug cartel. This cartel began when Mexican Army Special Forces deserters turned to the dark side. They were now threatening to cut off our heads and throw our bodies in the Rio Grande River. Adam said to me, "Now I know what a martyr feels like just before he dies." Grown men began to cry. If that wasn't bad enough, a black crow swooped in and perched on the top of the wall near us. Its presence was just another reminder of how dark and desperate our situation had become.

Without any sign of hope, suddenly a line from a popular song from the Jesus Movement dropped into my spirit. *He's my Rock, He's my Fortress, He's my Deliverer; in Him shall I trust.*[2] I started to sing it slowly to myself. Hope began to arise in my spirit. Then I sang it again, only louder. Confidence replaced hope. Finally, I sang it aloud with a boldness that every word of the song was true. I don't know if anyone understood what I was doing, but I knew God was with us.

As I looked at the bloodthirsty gang, I was drawn to the only female member. Our eyes made contact, and I sensed she knew something about my Jesus. Later, she identified me as a "good man" to the rest. Soon, for some unexplained reason, their demands began to subside. Miraculously, they decided to return all of our cell phones and money. Finally, they released us unharmed. We discovered later that they even escorted us to the border!

What we had witnessed was an example of heaven invading earth. Light had penetrated the darkness, and the darkness had to flee. The King and the angels of His Kingdom had come to our rescue, but the realization of His power had actually penetrated my life two years before. This book is the result of that life-changing encounter.

THE DARKNESS COMES

One day I received a phone call from a missionary friend of mine. Robert Duran had started an intensive training program for young Christian adults in Mexico called the Cave of Adullam. He and I had been friends for years, since back in the early '70s, when we had experienced true spiritual revival. He asked me to come down from Minnesota and teach for a week. Since my schedule was less than full, I accepted his invitation and headed to San Luis Potosi, Mexico.

When I arrived, I found the students engaging and the teaching fulfilling. I taught on the believer's marriage with Christ and His passion for the poor and disenfranchised. By Thursday night, I tried to get an early night's rest because the following day would be my last and I wanted to finish the week strong. I quietly drifted off to sleep, feeling grateful for my opportunity to share in the school. What I didn't realize was that God had prompted a particular student to pray that I would receive something special from Him before the next morning's class.

Suddenly, I woke up. I looked at the clock, and it said 4:00 AM. Instinctively, I closed my eyes, hoping to return quickly back to sleep. To my surprise, I received an unexpected vision from the Lord. It shook my spirit and awakened me completely. In the vision, I saw a map of the United States and Mexico. Covering the United States was a black darkness that appeared to be alive. Somehow, I knew it was poised to cross the Rio Grande River into Mexico. "What is this darkness?" I wondered. Almost as if there had been an audible voice, the answer came to my spirit with penetrating power and clarity. "Its name is *Babylon.*"

I jumped up and began looking for my notes and computer. The subject of Babylon had recently come up in my studies, but it lacked cohesiveness. Now, with renewed urgency, I went back to those Scriptures, asking myself, "What really is Babylon?" I discovered it appears over 250 times from Genesis to Revelation. The Bible calls Babylon a woman, a city, a land,

and a kingdom (see Rev. 17:3–5, 18:10; Isa. 39:3, 13:19). Finally, the Bible describes it as a mystery (see Rev. 17:5).

SEEKING THE SOURCE

While sitting perplexed on my bed with a Bible, laptop, and some scattered notes, I asked, "Where did Babylon come from, Lord?" My mind and spirit were now fully engaged. I sensed a need to go back to the earliest accounts in Genesis. I soon discovered that an evil king named Nimrod ruled over several cities in a plain called Shinar (see Gen. 10:10). He had a reputation as a powerful hunter, builder, and leader. Sadly, ambition, power, and pride also marked his life. The name Nimrod means "strong, rebel."[3] One of the most distinguished cities he ruled was Babel. The name Babel is the Hebrew form of the Greek name Babylon.[4] The Bible describes the world-changing building project that occurred there.

> And they said to one another, "Come, let us make bricks and burn them thoroughly." And they used brick for stone, and they used tar for mortar. And they said, "Come, let us build for ourselves a city, and a tower whose top will reach into heaven, and let us make for ourselves a name …" (Gen. 11:3–4 NASB).

This short narrative reveals three characteristics of Babylon that are foundational:

1. *Trust in human knowledge.* The builders of the city and the tower of Babel were very industrious. They revolutionized structure building by creating bricks to replace stones. This gave them virtually unlimited building materials that were easier to shape than stone and structurally sound. They also discovered a substance that would serve as mortar for the bricks.

2. *Independence.* The passage states that they wanted to build a tower that would *"reach into heaven."* They knew God was in heaven, and they decided they would be there too—*only without His help.*

3. *Pride.* It is obvious from the passage that pride was a prime motivator for the tower. The outcome of completing it would be to "make for our-

selves a name." Babylon reflected a faith in the supreme value of human knowledge, independence, and pride.

My troubling vision was beginning to make more sense. I began to feel the need to build upon this passage. I located some of my earlier notes on Revelation 17 and 18. In these chapters, it speaks of additional characteristics of Babylon.

> The name written on her forehead was a mystery: BABYLON THE GREAT THE MOTHER OF PROSTITUTES AND OF THE ABOMINATIONS OF THE EARTH. I saw that the woman was *drunk with the blood of God's holy people, the blood of those who bore testimony to Jesus. ... "The merchants of the earth will weep and mourn over her because no one buys their cargoes anymore*—cargoes of gold, silver, precious stones and pearls; fine linen, purple, silk and scarlet cloth; every sort of citron wood, and articles of every kind made of ivory, costly wood, bronze, iron and marble" (Rev. 17:5–6; 18:11–12).

Through these passages, the mystery of Babylon was becoming clearer. They reveal that Babylon also loves sexual pleasure outside of marriage. She hates those who follow God and has great influence over the wealth of this world.

As I read Isaiah 13 and Jeremiah 50 and 51, I also started to see what Babylon is not. Babylon is not the kingdom of darkness. It is heavily influenced by Satan's kingdom but Babylon's primary focus has always been the physical realm. I also do not believe it is "the flesh," which is used to describe internal desires opposed to the ways of God. This is because Babylon has always valued external appearances. The term "the world" comes close, but Babylon is more specific and has a definite spiritual component.

THE HEART OF THE BEAST

As I reflected on the basic characteristics of Babylon, I faced a troubling thought: *These are evident throughout the earth to various degrees. So why is the United States in blackness and not Mexico?* The answer again came quickly and powerfully into my spirit. "Mexico has not yet received the heart of Babylon."

"But what is its heart, Lord?" I asked.

In my spirit, I clearly heard the answer. The heart of Babylon declares, *"We do not need God."* This was the core danger.

I believe Babylon is actually a belief system based on the premise, *"We do not need God."* Babylon represents fallen humanity's desperate effort to establish its own universal value system. It is the kingdom of man independent of God. This kingdom seeks happiness and meaning without God's involvement. It is determined to reach its goals and develop its future without His leadership. Its citizens are not extreme atheists but common people whose lifestyles reflect an independence from the God of the Bible. Ironically, according to a recent poll, 92 percent of Americans believe in God,[5] so belief is not the issue. The problem is that we live as though we do not need Him!

We now live in a humanistic culture where the end of all things is the happiness of humankind.[6] Our currency states, "In God We Trust," but nothing could be further from the truth. We have been taught to trust in ourselves more than God. Tragically, we live as if He is no longer needed. Our abandonment of God and His influence has changed the very heart of our nation.

This new modern society has a place for the God of the Bible, but it is over there in the corner. It rejects Christian values and relies on the power of human intelligence to build a better world. Os Guinness once said, "Of all the cultures the church has lived in, the modern world is the most powerful, the most pervasive, and the most pressurizing. And it has done more damage to Christian integrity and effectiveness than all the persecutors of the church in history."[7]

ROCKED TO THE CORE

When people come to Christ for the first time, they experience a transformation of mind and heart. They see and understand spiritual realities formerly hidden from their comprehension. They walk from spiritual darkness into light. I experienced a similar epiphany at this time in my life. I have had wonderful experiences with God over the years, but this encounter with Him was very different. It came with such power and intensity that for more than a year, my spirit was inexplicably stirred. The Lord led me to reread the entire Bible with this different perspective. I was overwhelmed at times and found it difficult to share objectively what I was experiencing. A few times in prayer and meditation, I would double over with the burden of its implications. I am not exaggerating when I say this revelation has completely changed my view of this world and my role in it. Sin has never looked so evil and distasteful, and the danger to the Western Church has never appeared more ominous.

THE SEDUCTION

After considerable study, I have discovered that one of the kingdom of Babylon's greatest strengths is its power of seduction. Seduction comes from the word *seduce*, which means to lead astray, as from duty, to corrupt or to lead away from principles, faith, or allegiance.[8] The kingdom of Babylon's ambition is to lead good people away from the ways of God. It wants to rob them of biblical values by enticing them to embrace an appealing yet corrupted set of values.

I believe Proverbs 2 and 7 reveal one of the most vivid examples of this seduction. It is a metaphor of an adulterous woman who is sensual, crafty, defiant, wealthy, pleasure loving, and persuasive. These characteristics reflect the already-mentioned descriptions of Babylon. However, the passages reveal some additional key characteristics. This adulterous woman is everywhere; she will find you; and she claims you will not suffer any consequences if you become involved with her (see Prov. 7:12, 15, 19–20).

Today's advertising, entertainment media, and the Internet emulate these characteristics. Unrelenting sexual images and suggestions are inundating our airways, websites, and cable outlets. We have been seduced into believing we can engage in numerous forms of moral compromise and not suffer any consequences. Most observant Christians realize this but are unaware of the kingdom perpetuating it.

In addition, television and movies constantly portray a world that does not need God. Most television series offer a storyline where problems are resolved without His involvement. If we have cable or satellite transmission, then we are actually paying Babylon to have our minds and hearts subjected to constant seductive lies and absurd notions of a world existing successfully without God. The spiritually corrosive influence of entertainment media cannot be overestimated. Proverbs 2 and 7 reveal that assimilating this seductive world system results in death (see Prov. 2:18–19; 7:23). It is a universal truth established in eternity—the values of Babylon are never beneficial to our physical, mental, or spiritual health. They destroy life. The consequences may come quickly or over an extended period, but they will always bring us great harm. The apostle Peter warned the early Church of the empty claims by those who have become subjects of Babylon.

> For they mouth empty, boastful words and, by appealing to the lustful desires of the flesh, they entice people who are just escaping from those who live in error. They promise them freedom, while they themselves are slaves of depravity—for "people are slaves to whatever has mastered them" (2 Pet. 2:18–19).

THE OVERSHADOWING DARKNESS

As Babylon increases its influence, an *overshadowing darkness* begins to oppress individuals, families, neighborhoods, cities, and countries. This effect often leads to spiritual blindness. Those overshadowed frequently lose a sense of who they are. "But the way of the wicked is like deep darkness; they do not know what makes them stumble" (Prov. 4:19). When King Saul disobeyed the Lord, an overshadowing presence tormented him. The original text of 1 Samuel 16:14 suggests this presence choked and strangled Saul,[9] much like a wet blanket chokes a fire.

Even God's people suffer in this pervasive darkness. King David proclaimed, "The enemy pursues me, he *crushes me to the ground*; he makes me dwell in *darkness* like those long dead" (Ps. 143:3). Jesus experienced this overshadowing affect prior to His arrest in the garden of Gethsemane. "Every day I was with you in the temple courts, and you did not lay a hand on me. But this is *your hour—when darkness reigns*" (Luke 22:53). Later, when a cross bore our Savior, the physical realm became a reflection of the spiritual reality. "Now from the sixth hour *darkness fell* upon all the land until the ninth hour" (Matt. 27:45, NASB).

The early Church constantly faced the overshadowing influence of this corrupted value system. This kingdom not only blinded its subjects but also used them to spread its darkness. "The wrath of God is being revealed from heaven against all the godlessness and wickedness of men who *suppress* [to hold down][10] the truth by their wickedness" (Rom. 1:18). When the religious rulers faced the powerful words of truth spoken by the disciple Stephen, "They cried out with a loud voice, and stopped their ears, and ran *upon* [superimposition][11] him with one accord, And cast him out of the city, and stoned him ..." (Acts 7:57–58, KJV).

The urban neighborhood where I have worked for a decade has consistently experienced this type of phenomenon. There is something that you can feel when you visit there—especially in the spring. This may seem strange, but often we can tell when a shooting is imminent. We can feel it in the air. It seems there is something in the spirit realm demanding spilled blood. Local police are fighting a relentless battle to reduce crime. City planners have initiated improvements for the streets and businesses. The neighborhood has even received a community makeover. However, because the core problem is not physical; the spiritual overshadowing remains.

We are in a war today. Unfortunately, we are often focusing in the wrong direction. While many are scrutinizing political and economic decisions, the devil, or our moral weaknesses, we have missed an extremely formidable foe. Our lack of perception has allowed the kingdom of Babylon to infiltrate the foundations of our Christian faith. In this critical time in earth's history, we must awaken to this challenging reality and to God's overcoming light and power.

PRAYER

Oh God, save us from what we have become. We have been seduced by a system that appears so attractive, fashionable, and enticing, but it has corrupted our thinking and left our hearts stone cold. We have rebuked the darkness but still cannot see. We are unable to change unless this shroud of spiritual blindness is removed and Your light once again shines brightly in our hearts. Please, Lord, come in revelation power and love!

NOTES

1. George W. Bush, *UBR, Inc.*, http://www.people.ubr.com/authors/by-first-name/g/george-w-bush/george-w-bush-quotes/this-is-still-a.aspx (accessed 4/2/10).

2. Roy Hicks Jr. "Praise the Name of Jesus" (1976) http://www.musicnotes.com/sheetmusic/mtdVPE.asp?ppn=MN0059306 (accessed 11/16/10).

3. Albert Barnes, "Genesis 10:6–20" (from *Barnes' Notes*, Electronic Database Copyright © 1997, 2003, 2005, 2006 by Biblesoft, Inc. All rights reserved).

4. "Ancient Babylonia—History of Babylonia," *Bible History*, http://www.bible-history.com/babylonia/BabyloniaHistory_of_Babylonia.htm (accessed 11/16/10).

5. Adelle M. Banks, "Think You Know What Americans Believe about Religion? You Might Want to Think Again." *The Pew Forum on Religion and Public Life*. http://pewforum.org/news/display.php?NewsID=15907 (accessed 1/4/10).

6. Paris Reidhead, "Ten Shekels and a Shirt" (Minneapolis, MN: Bethany International, n.d.), http://www.sermonindex.net/ (accessed 3/10/10).

7. Os Guinness, *Prophetic Untimeliness* (Grand Rapids, MI: Baker Books, 2003), 51. Used by author's permission.

8. "Seduce,: *Dictionary.com*, http://dictionary.reference.com/browse/seduce (accessed 11/19/10).

9. *Jamieson, Fausset, and Brown Commentary*, Electronic Database (Biblesoft, Inc., 2006).

10. NT:2722 kate/xw *katecho* (kat-ekh'-o); from NT:2596 and NT:2192; to hold down (fast), in various applications (literally or figuratively), *Biblesoft's New Exhaustive Strong's Numbers and Concordance with Expanded Greek-Hebrew Dictionary*. Copyright © 1994, 2003, 2006 Biblesoft, Inc. and International Bible Translators, Inc.

11. NT:1909 e)pi/ **epi** (ep-ee'); a primary preposition; properly, meaning superimposition,(Biblesoft's New Exhaustive Strong's Numbers and Concordance with Expanded Greek-Hebrew Dictionary. Copyright © 1994, 2003, 2006 Biblesoft, Inc. and International Bible Translators, Inc.)

Chapter Notes

Chapter 2

RECIPE FOR DISASTER

Division is better than agreement in evil.
—GEORGE HUTCHESON[1]

By the rivers of Babylon we sat and wept when we remembered Zion.
—PSALM 137:1

B abylon possesses another tactical weapon, and it has to do with mixture. The Bible defines Babel as *confusion* in Genesis 11:9 but the word also means to *mingle*[2] or to *mix*.[3] Babylon has always been a mixture of cultures and values. Mixture often causes that which was clean and beneficial to become polluted and harmful. "Like a muddied spring or a polluted well are the righteous who give way to the wicked" (Prov. 25:26).

Alfred Nobel invented dynamite in 1867. It is a particularly powerful material and is composed of three parts nitroglycerin and one part diatomaceous earth. Nitroglycerin is a very unstable and explosive chemical, but diatomaceous earth is an organic and harmless compound. In fact, natural diatomaceous earth is often beneficial for insect pest control. Unfortunately, with the mixture of nitroglycerin, diatomaceous earth is transformed into a material that is very dangerous and can bring great harm to others.

There is a dangerous mixture occurring in our Church culture today. Under the banner of social relevance, we are accepting and esteeming the values of another kingdom that are opposed to God's ways. Much like Samson, we are losing our spiritual authority, power, and sight as the result of this contamination.

ISRAEL AND MIXTURE

In the wilderness, Jehovah gave ceremonial laws to the children of Israel. Such laws often prohibited the mixture of different substances. "Do not plant two kinds of seed in your vineyard; if you do, not only the crops you plant but also the fruit of the vineyard will be defiled. Do not plow with an ox and a donkey yoked together. Do not wear clothes of wool and linen woven together" (Deut. 22:9–11). To some, this may appear silly and unnecessary, but I believe God wanted to instill intolerance for mixture within the Hebrew culture. These instructions taught a much deeper spiritual principle. They were to be a separate and pure people, dedicated to God. Sadly, many refused to follow these commands.

The Children of Israel wanted to follow Jehovah but also adopt some of the customs of their neighbors. They wanted to intermarry, dabble in their neighbor's religions, and imitate the political systems they saw around them. They saw nothing dangerous with this mixture. "They didn't wipe out those godless cultures as ordered by God. Instead they intermarried with the heathen, and in time became just like them" (Ps. 106:34–35 MSG).

The Lord saw beyond Israel's desires for cultural freedom. He saw the false claims of neighboring broken kingdoms entrapping individuals, families, and the entire nation. He saw the soul ties that would result. He knew that their values would change and a different moral DNA would take root in their nation. The mixture would change everything. "Can a corrupt throne be allied with you—a throne that brings on misery by its decrees?" (Ps. 94:20).

Nearly every adult has had to confront cancer, either directly or indirectly. The way cancer operates in the body is quite remarkable. Cancer cells have different properties than regular cells. They have lost their ability to control their rate of division. They have become immortal and can grow indefinitely. Cancer cells are also able to invade adjacent normal cells and transform them into cancer cells.[4] This last characteristic is a particularly dangerous trait. Potentially, one cancer cell could invade one hundred healthy, normal cells and transform them into abnormal cancer cells.

Jehovah was not just concerned about false values and mindsets growing within a community. He saw the danger of a nation with Kingdom of God DNA becoming cancerous. He was concerned about the transformation of Israel's culture into a predatory, religious, self-serving system. Unfortunately, this is what we have in part of the Western Church today.

Because the Children of Israel refused to listen to the godly prophets, social and moral corruption resulted. But God, in His mercy, did not forsake them. When Israel's first king embraced many of the Babylonian values, God found a humble shepherd boy to reintroduce the importance of following the ways of Jehovah. After King David's righteous reign, his son Solomon came to power. Regrettably, Solomon neglected to follow the Lord with all his heart. He tried to be politically correct by tolerating other religions in their country. Under Solomon's leadership, anyone could freely worship other gods, including his own wives. This mixture in the land was not a sign of Israel's strength but of its weakness.

Many wicked kings followed Solomon, but even the more righteous ones had this problem. Asa, Jehoshaphat, and Joash failed to remove the high places of pagan worship. The attitude of Israel and Judah seemed to be summed up in the passage, "They worshiped the Lord but they also served their own gods ..." (2 Kings 17:33). Ironically, when Judah persisted in her rebellion against God and His Kingdom, judgment finally came in the form of captivity in the literal Babylon. There, they became enslaved to the degraded value system that so fascinated them. They had to drink the dregs of their foolish choices.

Once again, Jehovah extended mercy to the Hebrew nation. He delivered them from captivity and began to reintroduce the importance of serving Him exclusively. This culminated in the sending of His Son, Jesus, who vividly demonstrated the values and power of a greater Kingdom.

JESUS AND MIXTURE

In preparation for His earthly ministry, Jesus went into the wilderness to pray for forty days. While there, the prince of evil tried to cut Him a deal. "Again, the devil took him to a very high mountain and showed him all the kingdoms of the world and their splendor. 'All this I will give you,' he said, 'if you will bow down and worship me'" (Matt. 4:8–9). Notice that Jesus did not dispute the devil's claim of control over earthly kingdoms. The kingdoms of the world at that time had a common thread. They had a heart that declared, *"We do not need God."* They were all attempting to live without depending on Jehovah. But Jesus would not bow to Satan while also trying to honor His heavenly Father. He flatly refused a mixture of loyalty and devotion.

The Jewish people exhibited compelling interest when Jesus began to reach out with truth and love. Initially they followed Jesus because He healed the sick. However, after Jesus miraculously fed them, they became fixated on Him fulfilling their physical desires. They went from respecting His healing power to craving food and security. They were now more interested in what Jesus could do for them than what He had to say. If they could just make Him their king, He would be more obligated to provide for their needs. Jesus was aware of their mixed motives so He gave them the uncomfortable truth to weed out fakers from the true followers.

> Jesus answered, "Very truly I tell you, you are looking for me, not because you saw the signs I performed but because you ate the loaves and had your fill. Do not work for food that spoils, but for food that endures to eternal life, which the Son of Man will give you. On him God the Father has placed his seal of approval" (John 6:26–27).

Despite Christ's teaching and life demonstration, the early disciples also struggled with mixture. Even with their personal sacrifices, their motives remained mixed. "We left everything and followed you. What do we get out of it?" (Matt. 19:27 MSG). This same mixture affected the early Church. When Jesus appeared before the apostle John on the island of Patmos, He addressed the problem of mixture in the Laodicean church: "because you are lukewarm—neither hot nor cold—I am about to spit you out of my mouth" (Rev. 3:16). Lukewarm is the obvious mixture of hot and cold. Jesus was concerned with more than an absence of heat. He saw a mixed value system that had infected the life of that particular church.

KINGDOM DISORDER

It is interesting to note that Babylon is not just a physical kingdom. It has both a physical and spiritual component. Knowing how they interact is important. In the kingdom of Babylon, the physical realm is the end, and the spiritual realm becomes the means. Consequently, the kingdom of Babylon often seeks to use the spiritual realm to further its physical goals. Ambitious leaders often recognize a certain degree of additional power is available in the spirit world, and they want to harness this power to gain influence, health, and wealth. Judas used his spiritual position to garner physical gain. Peter recognized this dubious agenda when he warned Simon the Sorcerer, "May your money perish with you, because you thought you could buy the gift of God with money!" (Acts 8:20). Actually, Peter and the disciples were also guilty of using the spiritual to further the physical. Prior to Pentecost, they were hoping their association with the holy man Jesus would improve their personal status, ensure career advancement, and increase their country's political position.

IMPURE AND DEFILED RELIGION

James, the brother of Jesus, gave a clear description of true religion: "This is pure and undefiled religion in the sight of our God and Father, to visit orphans and widows in their distress, and to keep oneself unstained by the world" (James 1:27 NASB). True Christians will love the weak and be separated from this world's system.

Unfortunately, many Christians have become enticed by Babylon's form of religion. Much of today's preaching and teaching focuses on helping ourselves rather than God and others. We are constantly encouraged to use God as a means of obtaining material blessings. The emphasis is on earthly treasures rather than storing up treasures in heaven. It is a religious system that perpetuates selfishness.

I believe in the power of faith, but if material prosperity is our right then thankfulness and humility will be rare. When a church or ministry places a strong emphasis on physical possessions and money, it often reveals this form of Babylonian religion is in operation. The Bible warms us of this danger: "They think religion is a way to make a fast buck" (1 Tim. 6:5 MSG).

Another form of false religion attempts to solve the problem of human weakness through tighter control. It has incorporated legalistic rules to suppress our base appetites. It has suppressed women and demanded painful penance. It has created an environment of dishonesty and superficial righteousness. This form of religion has been very effective in pointing out what is wrong but is very inept at making things right. It is a world where mercy is minimized, neglected, or forgotten.

Jesus' greatest antagonists were the religious leaders. His death was largely because He dared to expose their deceptive beliefs and practices. The Bible attributes several characteristics to these misguided purveyors of false religion. Not surprisingly, many parallel the characteristics of the kingdom of Babylon. They were:

1. Prideful (Matt. 23:5–7)

2. Self-indulgent (Matt. 23:25)

3. Focused on external appearance (Mark 12:38)

4. Preying on the vulnerable (Mark 12:40)

5. Pious (Mark 12:40)

6. Lovers of money (Luke 16:14)

7. Greedy (Matt. 23:25)

8. Neglectful of justice, mercy, and faithfulness (Matt. 23:23)

9. Envious (Matt. 27:18)

10. Murderers of the righteous (Matt. 23:34–35)

In the time of Jesus, they offered answers to the inner need humans feel for spiritual reality and significance, but what they gave was shallow and demanding. They were unrelenting hucksters of a performance-based religion and perfected the art of spiritual abuse. Sadly, you can still find them around today.

Recently, while visiting my parents in central Minnesota, I learned that a devastating earthquake had rocked Haiti. It created unimaginable devastation. Days later, the rotting debris and undiscovered victims created a nauseating stench that heightened the misery of the survivors and rescue teams. After hearing and seeing yet another heartbreaking news report, my parents and I retired for the evening. That night, the Lord spoke a single sentence to my mother. Later, she had to search the dictionary to understand the full meaning. The Lord said, "Religion is *odious*." Odious means detestable, highly offensive, repugnant, and disgusting.[5] Babylon's impure and defiled religion reeks of death and decay.

KUMBAYA KINGDOM

For the last several years, the Western Church has made an effort to enhance its influence through increased social relevancy. This strategy has been particularly evident in the United States. However, in a quest for acceptance, the Church in America has lost something much more valuable. Once again, Os Guinness provides some critical insight:

> By our uncritical pursuit of relevance we have actually courted irrelevance; by our breathless chase after relevance without a matching commitment to faithfulness, we have become not only unfaithful but irrelevant; by our determined efforts to redefine ourselves in ways that are more compelling to the modern world than are faithful to Christ, we have lost not only our identity but our authority and relevance.[6]

I remember when the television series *American Idol* had an episode where all the finalists sang a popular Christian song. There was a lot of positive buzz in the Christian community. Christians encouraged themselves with this openness of the secular media. Nevertheless, it is important to realize that acknowledgment is not an *endorsement*. The kingdom of Babylon will

THE CLASH OF KINGDOMS

often tolerate some aspects of the Christian faith, but it is looking for something in return; it wants the Church to tolerate it. "I will record Rahab and Babylon among those who acknowledge me" (Ps. 87:4). This goes back to the builders of Babel and even the devil himself. The kingdom of Babylon is often willing to acknowledge God; it is just not willing to submit to Him or admit its need for Him.

THE ULTIMATE GOAL

What is the ultimate goal of the kingdom of Babylon? I believe its seductive mannerisms, overshadowing power, and intermingled nature is designed to ultimately lead to complete and absolute *domination*. This domination will control the way we live and think. This ultimately will include our families, our cities, our nations, and the world.

I believe you will know that it dominates when the culture operates in a manner that reflects its heart, *"We do not need God."* The nations who adopt this will be intolerant of those who are committed to the ways of God. True Christians who continue to declare their dependency on God will be threatened, punished, and eventually eliminated.

It is very important to consider the current influence of the kingdom of Babylon globally. Sadly, the entire world reflects a certain degree of domination. Besides cities and countries, there are specific regions of the world under its influence. Although changing, the basic status is:

- Today, in Europe, the kingdom of Babylon dominates the culture. The Church exists, but it has become largely institutionalized. Only a very small percentage of people are actively pursuing God. Currently, there are no community-transforming revivals occurring in this region. The continent is in a general state of spiritual decline and captivity. The nations are committed to independence, living their lives without God.

- The United States is only a few steps behind Europe. The Church is stronger and more evident than in Europe, but it has made a terrible error. It has tried to coexist with the kingdom of Babylon in an effort to become more prosperous and relevant. The result is no transforming revivals in any major city.

- The kingdom of Babylon has been gaining strength in parts of Latin America, Asia, and Africa, but these regions have yet to adopt its heart. Consequently, these areas of the world are experiencing transforming revivals today; hundreds are occurring simultaneously. This is where we should be watching, learning, and assisting, because they have the heart necessary for reformation in the Western Church.

This is my Father's world. O let me ne'er forget
That though the wrong seems oft so strong, God is the ruler yet.
This is my Father's world: the battle is not done:
Jesus Who died shall be satisfied,
And earth and Heav'n be one.[7]

NOTES

1.   George Hutcheson, *Grace Quotes*, http://thegracetabernacle.org/quotes/Evil-Fighting_it.htm (accessed 2/27/10).

2.   Albert Barnes, *Barnes' Notes*, Electronic Database (Biblesoft, Inc., 2006).

3.   *Biblesoft's New Exhaustive Strong's Numbers and Concordance with Expanded Greek-Hebrew Dictionary* (Seattle, WA: Biblesoft, Inc. and International Bible Translators, Inc., 2006).

4.   "Characteristics of Cancer Cells," http://www.microbiologyprocedure.com/viruses-and-cancer/characteristics-of-cancer-cells.htm (accessed 11/16/10).

5.   "Odious," *Dictionary.com,* http://dictionary.reference.com/browse/odious?&qsrc= (accessed 11/16/10).

6.   Os Guinness, *Prophetic Untimeliness* (Grand Rapids, MI: Baker Books, 2003), 15. Used by author's permission.

7.   Maltbie Babcock, "This is My Father's World" (1901), http://www.cyber-hymnal.org/htm/t/i/tismyfw.htm (accessed 5/12/10).

Chapter Notes

_____

_____

_____

_____

_____

_____

_____

_____

_____

_____

_____

_____

_____

_____

_____

Chapter 3

†he Magnificent Kingdom

It's the inside-outside, upside-down Kingdom, where you lose to
gain and you die to live.
—Misty Edwards[1]

The Lord has established his throne in heaven, and his kingdom rules over all.
—Psalm 103:19

The subject of God's Kingdom was never a side issue to Jesus. It was
the centerpiece of His teaching. He spoke of the Kingdom of God
more than any other subject. It was the first thing He preached
in His earthly ministry (see Matt. 4:17). It was the last thing He preached
prior to His ascension (see Acts 1:3). In between, He mentions it over one
hundred times! He delivered the message of God's Kingdom with authority
and without compromise. He was not interested in enhancing the current
religious and cultural value system with new ideas and modifications. He
was presenting a very different way of living. It was a pure, unadulterated
message without mixture. So central was the message that Jesus was the
visible representation of the Kingdom He preached.

The major theme of His parables was the Kingdom of God. He often began by declaring, "The Kingdom of heaven is like …":

1. A man who sowed good seed in his field (Matt. 13:24).

2. A mustard seed (Matt. 13:31).

3. Yeast in flour (Matt. 13:33).

4. Treasure hidden in a field (Matt. 13:44).

5. A merchant looking for fine pearls (Matt. 13:45).

6. A net that caught all kinds of fish (Matt. 13:45).

7. The owner of a house with old and new treasures (Matt. 13:52).

8. A king who wanted to settle his accounts (Matt. 18:23).

9. A landowner who hired some workers (Matt. 20:1).

10. A king who threw a wedding banquet (Matt. 22:2).

11. Ten virgins and a bridegroom (Matt. 25:1).

12. A man who went on a journey (Matt. 25:1).

I think you get the point. There are twelve separate and unique parables regarding God's Kingdom found in the gospel of Matthew alone! Besides the study of the nature and character of God, the Kingdom of God is the deepest and most profound subject we can explore. At first glance, the Kingdom may appear to be a simple and straightforward subject, but its nature and character may very well take more than a lifetime for a follower of Christ to absorb.

When the disciples asked Jesus how to pray, Jesus taught them the most famous prayer in history. "Our Father in heaven, hallowed be your name, *your kingdom come*, your will be done on earth as it is in heaven. Give us today our daily bread…" (Matt. 6:9–11). What is significant but often overlooked is that Jesus wanted His followers to pray for the Kingdom to come even before asking for help with their personal needs. That differs from most contemporary prayers.

The Kingdom was so important that Jesus said we must seek it before anything else. "But seek first his kingdom and his righteousness, and all these things will be given to you as well" (Matt. 6:33). Can you imagine that? Jesus tells us to make His Kingdom the primary focus in our lives, and as we do, He will meet our needs. This too is very different from modern-day Christianity.

Jesus said that preaching the Kingdom was the purpose of His coming. "I must preach the kingdom of God to the other cities also, because for this purpose I have been sent" (Luke 4:43 NKJV). When Jesus sent out His disciples, He directed them to preach the Kingdom of God (see Luke 9:1–2). After Pentecost, Phillip experienced great success as he declared the Kingdom of God (see Acts 8:12). Throughout the apostle Paul's missionary journeys, including his historic visit to Rome, he argued persuasively about the Kingdom of God (see Acts 19:8, 28:30–31).

All followers of Christ must also understand the importance of spreading God's Kingdom to their families, communities, and nation or they will miss their critical mission on earth. Why are so many people struggling with sin? They have not received the Kingdom. Why do Christians have such few encounters with God? They are not focusing on His Kingdom.

Why do so many Christians feel powerless to change their families and community? They do not understand the Kingdom of God.

The Mysterious Kingdom

Jesus had an interesting discussion with a religious ruler one evening. Once again, He spoke about the Kingdom of God in contrast to the other kingdom. He taught that one relied upon visible evidence and human knowledge while the other relied upon spiritual evidence and the knowledge of God. Jesus explained to Nicodemus, "You should not be surprised at my saying, 'You must be born again.' The wind blows wherever it pleases. You hear its sound, but you cannot tell where it comes from or where it is going. So it is with everyone born of the Spirit" (John 3:7–8).

The Kingdom of God is much like the wind. The wind is tangible but often invisible. You can monitor it, but you cannot contain it. The wind does not reveal where it came from and where it is going. Our intellectual efforts and scientific methods cannot control it. You cannot dissect the wind or chemically analyze a pound of it. Jesus declared, "The kingdom of God does not come with observation; nor will they say, 'See here!' or 'See there!' For indeed, the kingdom of God is within you" (Luke 17:20–21 NKJV). The Kingdom becomes a part of us when we become a part of the Kingdom.

The Scripture also tells us in Matthew 13:33 that the Kingdom of God is like yeast. Albert Barnes explains:

> It is secret, silent, steady; pervading all the faculties of the soul and all the kingdoms of the world, as leaven, or yeast, though hidden in the flour, and though deposited only in one place, works silently until all the mass is brought under its influence.[2]

The action of the Kingdom of God is invisible to the naked eye but totally transforming in what it touches. Its effects are very evident, even if the activity is unseen.

Besides Nicodemus, there was another Bible character whose actions revealed her ignorance of the Kingdom of God. "'Then the mother of Zebedee's sons came to Jesus with her sons and, kneeling down, asked a favor of him. 'What is it you want?' he asked. She said, 'Grant that one of these two sons of mine may sit at your right and the other at your left in your kingdom'" (Matt. 20:20–21). Jesus' response was surprisingly direct and to the point, "You don't know what you are asking" (Matt. 20:22). In essence, Jesus told her she had no idea what the Kingdom was or what it involved.

Saul of Tarsus also thought he understood God's Kingdom. After all, he had carefully obeyed the Law and rabbinical teachings and became a distinguished Pharisee. He thought he possessed clear spiritual vision, but he was actually blind. Therefore, God had to make him physically blind on the road to Damascus so that he could finally obtain true spiritual vision. Saul was like the Western Church—religious but blind to the Kingdom of God.

THE KINGDOM REVEALED

Here is a mistake many make. *The Kingdom of God is not the Church.* It has always been more than the Church. The King of kings has commissioned the Church to represent Him and His Kingdom. For many years, we have focused so much on the Church that we have neglected His Kingdom. "If the Church takes you beyond itself to the feet of Christ and His Kingdom, it is beautiful. But if it stops you and makes itself the issue, then it is not beautiful. It is idolatrous."[3] The Church's validity is contingent on its loyalty to God's Kingdom.

So what is the Kingdom? It is God's ultimate program for our spiritual and physical life. It is the ideal way of living based on a perfect set of values. It is not just a better way; it is the *only* proper way to live. Its values are universal and inhabit eternity. These Kingdom values provide the necessary structure and purpose for our lives. If we yield to these values, our physical, psychological, and spiritual life become stable and healthy. If we resist, our body, soul, and spirit suffer—plain and simple. We were designed to live according to its ways.

Jesus demonstrated, through His life, the superiority of God's Kingdom. Two thousand years ago, within the bosom of a little baby in a barnyard manger, God offered a revolutionary blueprint for living. He later demonstrated and declared that this Kingdom blueprint *was* the gospel (see Matt. 24:14). Jesus came to die for our sins, but salvation was only the beginning. The Good News is more than confessing our sins and accepting Christ as our Savior. It is escaping the clutches of a fallen kingdom and being born again into His Kingdom.

In the first-century Church, they understood this. To them, baptism was a public declaration of a change in citizenship. They were abandoning their loyalty to one kingdom and embracing the values and leadership of another Kingdom. They wanted to demonstrate their change of life quickly and publicly. This is why the person who led them to Christ often baptized them immediately after conversion (see Matt. 28:19). Today, Christianity is being offered but without a change of kingdoms.

Many today are writing and singing about the Kingdom of God. Unfortunately, it is often people's attempt to tap into spiritual resources to build their own kingdom. The only real way we can be a part of God's Kingdom is by surrendering our own building plans. The Kingdom does not exist to further our ideas or ambitions. The King wants to awaken us to our role in the expansion of His Kingdom.

If you don't plan to live the Christian life totally committed to knowing your God and to walking in obedience to Him, then don't begin; for this is what Christianity is all about. It is a change of citizenship, a change of governments, and a change of allegiance. If you have no intention of letting Christ rule your life, then forget Christianity; it's not for you.[4]

The early Church knew that this was more than a future Kingdom in heaven. This was something to embrace and expand now. When Jesus spoke of it, He often used the present tense. "Time's up! *God's kingdom is here.* Change your life and believe the Message" (Mark 1:13 MSG). Later He stated, "But if it's by God's power that I am sending the evil spirits packing, then *God's kingdom is here for sure*" (Matt. 12:28).

WE NEED GOD!

Unlike the kingdom of Babylon, those committed to the values of the Kingdom of God declare, without reservation, *"We need God!"* Not surprisingly, those with physical, educational, and financial limitations are more inclined to embrace this creed. The most needy and hungry seem to find God's Kingdom more readily.

> Consider your calling, brethren, that there were not many wise according to the flesh, not many mighty, not many noble; but God has chosen the foolish things of the world to shame the wise, and God has chosen the weak things of the world to shame the things which are strong, and the base things of the world and the despised, God has chosen, the things that are not, that He might nullify the things that are, that no man should boast before God (1 Cor. 1:26–29 NASB).

The problem today is that many view dependency as a weakness. Our affirming society has built up an aura of self-sufficiency. We elevate our giftedness and competence. We seek to overcome through our own abilities. We desire to be strong and self-assured and falsely assume that God can most readily use the gifted and capable.

KINGDOM ORDER

Like Babylon, the Kingdom of God has both a spiritual and physical component. "Jesus answered, 'Very truly I tell you the truth, no one can enter the kingdom of God unless he is born of water and the Spirit. Flesh gives birth to flesh, but the Spirit gives birth to spirit'" (John 3:5–6). The difference is that in the Kingdom of God, the spiritual realm is the end, and the physical realm becomes the means. Consequently, the physical serves the spiritual. The physical realm is not evil, as Gnostics would claim;[5] it is just temporal and imperfect.

Regrettably, many of those who followed Jesus were preoccupied with fulfilling their physical desires. Jesus presented an alternative perspective, "The Spirit gives life; the flesh counts for nothing …" (John 6:63). "Whoever wants to be my disciple must deny themselves and take up their cross and follow me. For whoever wants to save their life will lose it, but whoever loses their life for me will find it. What good will it be for someone to gain the whole world, yet forfeit their soul? Or what can anyone give in exchange for their soul?" (Matt. 16:24–26).

Furthermore, when there is a loss in the physical realm that brings advancement in the spiritual realm, it is not a setback. Ultimately, we may discover blessings in both realms, but the spiritual must be the priority. "And do not set your heart on what you will eat or drink; do not worry about it. For the pagan world runs after all such things, and your Father knows that you need them. But *seek his kingdom*, and these things will be given to you as well" (Luke 12:29–31). We need to pause and consider the implications of this simple but radical aspect of the Kingdom of God. This alone can change the very way we live our lives.

In Matthew 26, we see two people representing two contrasting value systems. Prior to Christ's dark night of the soul, He received an unexpected visitor. A woman with an alabaster box of expensive perfume came to anoint Him and in doing so, prepared His body for burial. This woman reflected the values of the Kingdom of God. She recognized that the physical realm serves the spiritual realm. She sacrificed something of great physical value to honor someone of even greater spiritual value. The narrative then quickly shifts to Judas. He reflected the contrary values of the kingdom of Babylon. Judas was more than willing to make spiritual compromises for physical gain. His treacherous plot revealed a heart that desired a physical increase more than a spiritual increase.

Jesus consistently reflected the values of His Father's Kingdom, as "he was so very rich, yet to help you he became so very poor, so that by being poor he could make you rich" (2 Cor. 8:9 TLB). He faced the cruelty of the cross without fear of physical loss but with the hope of our spiritual gain. This perspective and position is why the first-century Church was also willing to face torture and death. This perspective and attitude is rare today. In troubled times, many Christians are quick to store up resources that support their physical rather than their spiritual lives. The focus is backward. Preparation can be prudent but an overemphasis on our physical well-being is not.

ENTERING THE NO-SPIN ZONE

The kingdom of Babylon is the original spin zone. It gains many of its followers through seduction and deception. Conversely, the beautiful aspect of the Kingdom of God is that it rules by truth rather than half-truths and misrepresentations. The book of Proverbs contrasts the two kingdoms' cultures. We have already looked at the adulterous woman in Proverbs 2 and 7, but the Scriptures also reveal a woman called Wisdom in Proverbs 1 and 8. She cries out:

> Listen, for I have trustworthy things to say; I open my lips to speak what is right. My mouth speaks what is true, for my lips detest wickedness. All the words of my mouth are just; none of them is crooked or perverse. To the discerning all of them are right; they are upright to those who have found knowledge. Choose my instruction instead of silver, knowledge rather than choice gold (Prov. 8:6–10).

In direct contrast to the adulterous woman, Wisdom states, "I hate pride and arrogance, evil behavior and perverse speech" (Prov. 8:13). Finally, rather than death, Wisdom proclaims, "whoever finds me finds life and receives favor from the Lord" (Prov. 8:35).

Truth is a core value and a reflection of the Kingdom of God. Jesus said, "I am the way and the truth and the life ..." (John 14:6). Along with a declaration of fact, it was a direct challenge to the seductive lies of Babylon. Seventy-eight times Jesus said, "I tell you the truth." Those who are part of God's Kingdom must also be committed to truth. "Behold, you desire truth in the inner parts" (Ps. 51:6 NKJV). "I have no greater joy than to hear that my children are walking in the truth" (3 John 4).

PRINCIPLE OF PENETRATION

The Kingdom of God rules by love, but that love is not passive. "The kingdom of heaven has been *forcefully advancing*, and forceful men lay hold of it" (Matt. 11:12, NIV1984). "Forcefully advancing" denotes "to crowd oneself into."[6] Unlike the overshadowing presence of Babylon, the Kingdom of God has an innate ability to *penetrate* darkness, regardless of its strength or size. The very nature of the Kingdom of God is to penetrate all other kingdoms and to bring freedom to its captives. In Scripture, we have metaphors of salt penetrating meat and water penetrating soil, but there is something more intriguing. By nature, the Kingdom of God *replaces* what it penetrates. Consequently, the Kingdom of God is more like light and wind. Light not only penetrates darkness but also it replaces it (see Ps. 94:1–2). Wind penetrates a structure through an open door or window and then replaces the atmosphere that once existed there (see Ps. 68:1–2).

CHEMISTRY 101

One day, when I was in my mid-teens, I had a wild idea. I decided to make some hydrogen balloons. Most of us are familiar with the helium balloons used in birthday parties, but hydrogen is much lighter and therefore more dramatic. I wanted to see just how buoyant a hydrogen balloon would be. But there was one major problem—it is very explosive. I was able to figure out how to make hydrogen by using chemicals found in a drain cleaner. Soon I had a small lab set up in our downstairs bathroom.

I set a one-gallon jug on the toilet lid and corked it with a line going to another one-gallon jug filled with water, which was inverted in the bathroom sink. Once the reaction started, the gas expanded from one jug and began to replace the water in the other. When finished, I used a cork with two lines to seal the inverted gallon jug filled with hydrogen. One line went to the water faucet, while the other went to a deflated balloon. As I would turn the water on, it would flow into the jug and force the hydrogen out into the balloon. The point is that first the gas penetrated and replaced the water in the jug, and later the water penetrated and replaced the gas in the jug. This is penetration and replacement.

That foray into unsanctioned science reached an untimely end when the drain cleaner reaction broke the jar, causing a China Syndrome[7] on the toilet seat. This meltdown was impossible to hide from my exasperated mom. In addition, I had one other problem. I had filled all my balloons, but some hydrogen remained trapped in the jug. I decided to take the cap off and just release the gas. Since I was sixteen at the time and still a bit naive, I decided to place a match over the opening to see if there was any remaining hydrogen. The ensuing explosion created a concussion that literally shook the entire house. Fortunately, the "penetration" of exploding hydrogen wasn't enough to cause a "replacement" of our house!

ASSIGNMENT: PENETRATE AND REPLACE

This fascinating principle of kingdom penetration has its roots in Genesis. In the twelfth chapter, we see that God directed Abram to leave the country of Haran to go to an unfamiliar land called Canaan. Why Canaan? To gain understanding, we must go back to the days of Noah. After the flood, Noah hung up his ark-building tools and became a farmer. One of the first things he planted was a vineyard. We can only speculate on how familiar Noah was with the properties of the resulting wine. The Scriptures only tell us that one night Noah became drunk and naked. His youngest son, Ham, discovered his father's condition and told his older brothers. The older brothers took action and covered their father's shame. Unlike Ham, they did something to correct the problem. When Noah became sober, he blessed his older sons but cursed Ham's youngest son, whose name was Canaan (see Gen. 9:25–27). Years later, Canaan's descendants migrated and settled in the land that became known as Canaan.

Now God was calling righteous Abram to penetrate the land of that specific curse and replace it with a blessing. Talk about penetrating and replacing. When Abram settled in the new land, God changed his name to Abraham. This new name ironically now included the name "ham"—the disrespectful father of Canaan! A superior Kingdom had now penetrated and replaced the curse and its kingdom. Abraham's obedience had essentially transformed the land from a cursed place to a place of abundance.

Perhaps some would argue that the devil knew God's redemptive plan for the land of Canaan and therefore influenced a cursed people to move there. If so, the plan failed miserably. Regardless, God penetrated Canaan's pitiful condition through Abraham and revealed His glory and power. This spiritual dynamic is not isolated. In every revival, God penetrates and replaces territory that has become spiritually accursed. He then transforms it into a place of abundance. This is His nature and the nature of His Kingdom.

Years later, when God led the Children of Israel from Egypt to the Promised Land, it was described as "a good and spacious land, a land flowing with milk and honey ..." (Ex. 3:8). Abraham's obedience had brought a blessing to the land, but it remained occupied by the followers of another kingdom. Through Joshua's leadership, the Children of Israel were able to penetrate the land and replace its inhabitants.

Kingdom penetration appeared again when Israel struggled under the leadership of its first king. God's presence filled King Saul initially, but because of disobedience, the overshadowing power of Babylon often oppressed him. Panic attacks and senseless rage characterized his condition. God initiated a plan for resolving the problem. The solution came in the form of a humble shepherd boy. Young David brought the Kingdom of God into King Saul's throne room. There, David played his harp, and his Kingdom-inspired worship music penetrated and replaced the darkness.

The book of Acts illustrates several examples of the Kingdom of God penetrating the kingdom of Babylon. This was the role of the early Church in cities throughout Asia and Europe. This salient characteristic is what makes the Church of today so different and so much less influential. *Today's culture is also broken. However, Jesus is not calling us to fix it. He is calling us to penetrate and replace it!*

Several years ago, our ministry looked for a facility in the urban core that would be an accessible link to the poor and disenfranchised. Of all the empty storefronts available, the one we chose was a former pornographic video store. Only later did we discover that godly intercessors had prayed that the former business would close and that something for God's Kingdom would take its place. With a foundation of prayer, we cleaned and remodeled the facility to create a new ministry center and coffee shop. With each step, we saw the fulfillment of those prayers. We were part of the penetration of one kingdom and the establishment of another. We were fulfilling our spiritual purpose and destiny!

PRAYER

Lord, in this desperate hour, we need You, and we need Your Kingdom. Come, oh matchless King, and reign over us with eternal wisdom and love. May Your Kingdom become established once again in our communities and nation. We long for it to penetrate and replace all that has led Your people into spiritual captivity. Help us to seize every daily opportunity to bring Your Kingdom where we live and work. Give us a renewed sense of spiritual destiny and purpose!

NOTES

1.   Misty Edwards, "Servant of All," *Onething Live 2006* (2007).

2.   Albert Barnes, *Barnes' Notes*, Electronic Database (Biblesoft, Inc., 2006).

3.   E. Stanley Jones, *The Unshakable Kingdom and the Unchanging Person* (New York: Abingdon Press, 1972), 145.

4.   K. Arthur, quoted in *Revival Quotes*, http://www.evanwiggs.com/revival/fireham/Revival%20Quotes.htm (accessed 1/4/10).

5.   "Gnostic," *Knowledgerush*, http://www.knowledgerush.com/kr/encyclopedia/Gnostic/ (accessed 5/12/10).

6.   T:971 bia/zw *biazo* (bee-ad'-zo); from NT:979; to force, i.e. (reflexively) to crowd oneself (into), or (passively) to be seized: *Biblesoft's New Exhaustive Strong's Numbers and Concordance with Expanded Greek-Hebrew Dictionary.* Copyright © 1994, 2003, 2006 Biblesoft, Inc. and International Bible Translators, Inc.

7.   A hypothetical nuclear-reactor accident in which the fuel would melt through the floor of the containment structure and burrow into the earth. *Dictionary.com*, http://dictionary.reference.com/browse/China+Syndrome?&qsrc= (accessed 11/16/10).

Chapter Notes

Chapter 4

His Beautiful Kingdom Values

It is a great pleasure to live with positive hope that the most
deprived will gain access into the Kingdom of God.
—MATHIEU KEREKOU[1]

People will come from east and west and north and south, and
will take their places at the feast in the kingdom of God.
—LUKE 13:29

D o you remember choosing sides for a pick-up basketball game
when you were young? I remember I was often one of the last
kids chosen because I was shorter than most. I came to expect
it, but it always made me feel less valuable than the rest of the guys. There
are many people today who do not feel very special. They work hard and try
their best but always seem to come up short. There are winners and losers in
this life, but many feel more like losers. Amazingly, when Christ came, He
took people who considered themselves losers and made them His world-
changers. He did this by making them citizens of a superior Kingdom.

Romans 14:17–18 declares that the Kingdom of God consists of righteousness, peace, and joy in the Holy Spirit. These values are in direct contrast to the kingdom of Babylon. The kingdom of Babylon often esteems things the Kingdom of God despises (see Luke 16:15). Babylon touts certain components for success, but God's Kingdom largely ignores them. The Kingdom of God consists of a set of values far superior to those representing Babylon.

IRRELEVANT AGE

God's Kingdom does not show favoritism to what our society favors—young adults who are athletic, beautiful, and confident. In the Kingdom of God, a person's age is irrelevant. When God wants to do something and needs someone to play a role in it, He does not disqualify people because of their age. It is not because He is committed to be an equal opportunity employer. It is because it just does not matter.

When God told Abraham to leave his country for the land of Canaan, Abraham was already seventy-five years old. Moses was eighty years old when God directed him to lead the Hebrew nation out of Egypt and into the Promised Land. Noah was over five hundred years old when God first told him to build the ark! These senior citizens were no lightweights in God's Kingdom. They did not allow their age to keep them from their spiritual calling and purpose.

When God wanted to raise up a prophet to lead the Children of Israel, He chose a young boy named Samuel. Years later, Samuel anointed a young, overlooked shepherd boy named David to become king of Israel. When Judah faced the reality of captivity, God chose young Jeremiah to be a prophet to the nation. Jeremiah objected because he thought his age disqualified him. "'Ah, Sovereign Lord,' I said, 'I do not know how to speak; I am too young.' But the Lord said to me, 'Do not say, "I am too young." You must go to everyone I send you to and say whatever I command you. Do not be afraid of them, for I am with you and will rescue you,' declares the Lord" (Jer. 1:6–8).

One time, our family attended a Christian conference in Kansas City, Missouri. When we returned to our hotel, my seven-year-old grandson,

Jason, rode the elevator with my daughter, Molly. Also on the elevator was another conference attendee. This teenager introduced himself to Jason. "My name is Alex, and God has given me the gift to be able to see light and dark coming from a person. I noticed so much light coming from you that I would like to pray with you." He then prayed for young Jason—that the light God gave him would always be there. Alex's prayer was very sincere. When he finished, he started to say goodbye, but then Jason asked to pray for him. Alex was surprised at seven-year-old Jason's offer!

Jason then began, "Jesus, I pray that You will take away all the fear Alex has that he is going to die. Please remind him that You will keep him here until he has done everything that You need him to do. Thank You, God, for Alex and just please take away all his fear, Lord." When Jason finished praying, Alex fell to his knees. He looked in shock for a few seconds and then began to share something amazing with Jason and Molly. He told them that fear had haunted him his whole life. He never slept through the night because he was afraid he would die in his sleep. Even after giving his life to the Lord just a few months prior, he was still struggling with the fear of dying prematurely. He now knew God had revealed to Jason something that only he and his mother knew. He felt like God had set him free, but the true test would be going to bed that night!

We saw Alex the next morning, and he was on cloud nine! He was going around telling everyone that the Lord used a little boy to set him free. His mother, Crystal, came to Molly and emotionally expressed her thanks and praise to God. She told Molly that her son had never slept through the night for fear of dying—until last night!

One of the reasons that age is irrelevant is because time is not an issue. "But do not forget this one thing, dear friends: With the Lord a day is like a thousand years, and a thousand years are like a day" (2 Pet. 3:8). Regarding the length of the disciple John's life, Jesus said to the others, "What is that to you?" (John 21:22). In other words, He was saying, "This really is not important."

God is as comfortable using someone young, middle-aged, or old. In His Kingdom, it just does not matter. This truth can be very comforting and empowering if we grasp it—especially if we happen to be younger than eighteen or older than sixty-five. Our society and the kingdom of Babylon overvalue young and talented adults while undervaluing other age groups. "In the last days, God says, I will pour out my Spirit on *all people*. Your sons and daughters will prophesy, your young men will see visions, your old men will dream dreams" (Acts 2:17). We may hear prophetic proclamations regarding the younger generation, but Jesus used the term "generation" to describe the current age rather than a specific age group. In His Kingdom, He wants every age group to be involved.

INCONSEQUENTIAL INTELLIGENCE

God is the most intelligent being in the universe, but human intelligence is not a core value in the Kingdom of God. The Bible puts it into perspective: "Let not the wise man boast of his wisdom…but let him who boasts boast about this: that he understands and knows me…" (Jer. 9:23-24 NIV1984). Today there is a strong emphasis on education. This has some merit, but we must keep it in perspective. The early Church did not consist of seminary graduates directed by an intelligent denominational structure. Simple, ordinary people who had experienced something extraordinary, championed this world-changing movement. When these early disciples embarked on an evangelistic campaign in Jerusalem, some very frustrated religious leaders determined to stop them. "When they saw the courage of Peter and John and realized that they were *unschooled, ordinary men*, they were astonished and they took note that these men had been with Jesus" (Acts 4:13).

One early Church exception was the apostle Paul. He was a brilliantly educated man, yet he would be the first to admit that his intelligence was inconsequential in his effectiveness. "My message and my preaching were not with wise and persuasive words, but with a demonstration of the Spirit's power" (1 Cor. 2:4). Paul recognized that the power of the Holy Spirit was the most important component for success.

Charles Finney, the great revivalist of the nineteenth century, made an astute observation regarding the rapid spread of Christianity throughout the United States at the time. He drew a distinction between the bureaucratic denominations and the informal Methodist movement that was gaining influence and popularity.

> Look at the Methodists. Many of their ministers are unlearned, in the common sense of the term—many of them taken right from the shop or farm, and yet they have gathered congregations, and pushed their way, and won souls everywhere. Wherever the Methodists have gone, their plain, pointed and simple, but warm and animated, mode of preaching has always gathered congregations.[2]

The common perception today is that a person must be educated to be effective in expanding the Kingdom, but experience has proven otherwise.

> It is a fact worthy of note that those converts who are most eager to propagate the faith of Christ are frequently the men who have received least education at our hands.[3] ... It ought to be a cardinal principle with missionaries that anyone who knows enough to be saved by Christ knows enough to tell another how he may be saved.[7]

I worked in the missions department of a Christian organization for several years. During my tenure, over one hundred career missionaries completed an exclusive survey. One of the findings was quite enlightening: a bachelor's degree or graduate degree in theology did not mean greater success at winning people to Jesus Christ. Education was apparently not an essential prerequisite for expanding the Kingdom of God.

IMMATERIAL MONEY

God owns the cattle on a thousand hills (see Ps. 50:10), but He has a different perspective on riches than the prevailing culture. When Jesus saw that many who had followed Him were hungry, He directed His disciples to feed them. They protested, "That would take more than half a year's wages! Are we to go and spend that much on bread and give it to them to eat?" (Mark 6:37). They felt helpless because of the financial resources involved. When the temple taxes needed to be paid, Jesus did not panic. He simply instructed the disciples to catch a fish and remove the coin from its mouth.

Initially, the disciples had trouble adjusting to Jesus' view of finances. However, after Pentecost, the Church turned the world upside down without any major funding sources. Many had little disposal income. "Peter said, 'Silver or gold I do not have ...'" (Acts 3:6). They proved, dramatically, that in the expansion of God's Kingdom, you do not need a lot of money. Yet, today the consensus in the Western Church and missions is that we are helpless without it.

> It is difficult to express the sense of overwhelming materialism which a prolonged and careful study of our missionary literature produces upon the mind of the reader. Careful examination reveals very few articles which do not contain, directly or indirectly, an appeal for money. It is "money" "money" everywhere, all the time; everything depends upon money.[5]

Everywhere you turn, churches and ministries are in need of money. If Christians are doing a work for God and the money stops coming, then they instinctively attempt to gain new sources of income. If that fails, they assume God is no longer in it. The conclusion is clear—most Christians feel powerless without money.

Finances are an issue but much more with us than with God. I have a friend from Africa who pastors a church in America. He once shared with me about a man who came to him and said he would like to support his ministry. The man pulled out his checkbook and wrote out a check for three million dollars! My pastor friend accepted it but disregarded the check for a couple of days, thinking it was a joke. Finally, my friend's wife suggested that he try to deposit it in the bank. To his shock, the check cleared. Later, he asked the Lord why He would give him such a large amount. The Lord said that they simply did not need it up in heaven!

UNNECESSARY BEAUTY

God appreciates beauty. When He created the heavens and the earth, He looked at it and described it as being excellent in every way (see Gen. 1:31 TLB). The garden of Eden was the most beautiful paradise on earth. In heaven, Jesus is preparing a place for those who love Him. This too is a beautiful place. Nevertheless, physical beauty is not a core value in His Kingdom. Consequently, He does not judge someone's worth by his or her physical appearance.

A few years ago, NBC's *Dateline* did a story on whether physical appearance matters. The piece drew on the experience of Dr. Gordon Patzer, who has spent thirty years studying and writing about physical attractiveness. The results were quite revealing. "A person's physical attractiveness—the look that they're basically born with—impacts every individual literally from birth to death … People are valued more who are higher in physical attractiveness. As distasteful as that might be, that's the reality," according to Dr. Patzer.[6]

Using a variety of tests you would see in normal, everyday life, they were able to confirm many of Dr. Patzer's findings. They discovered that strangers who possessed higher physical attractiveness were assisted much more readily. They also determined that they were automatically trusted more. The power of physical beauty became apparent in some surprising ways. "We see in medical interactions, patients who go to physicians, and those of higher physical attractiveness, the physicians will spend more time with that person and will also spend more time answering individual questions that that person asked," says Dr Patzer. "In fact, even justice is not blind to beauty. Studies have shown that juries find arguments more persuasive if they're made by attractive lawyers."[7]

Our culture is obsessed with becoming as attractive as possible. Possessing good looks will often help a person's career, and lacking it may possibly hurt it. Many assume Jesus possessed better than average looks. Artists have often depicted Jesus this way, but the portrayal is likely unscriptural. Isaiah states, "He had no beauty or majesty to attract us to him, nothing in his appearance that we should desire him" (Isa. 53:2).

Some claim you cannot judge a book by its cover. Nowhere is this more evident than in the Kingdom of God. In His Kingdom, physical appearance is not a qualifying component. The Lord revealed to the prophet Samuel that a young shepherd boy would someday replace the imposing King Saul, "Do not consider his appearance or his height, for I have rejected him. The Lord does not look at the things people look at. People look at the outward appearance, but the Lord looks at the heart" (1 Sam. 16:7).

The Kingdom of God is not an exclusive club for people who are beautiful and handsome. Rather, it is a collection of mostly ordinary-looking people. God does not consider our outward appearance when it comes to loving us, but He is constantly attracted to the beauty of our hearts. My eleven-year-old granddaughter understood this when she wrote these words following a prayer meeting.

I may not have the best clothes or even have the cutest hair; but through God, I am beautiful. Through God, I am a shining light. You may see me all messed up, but all He sees is the most beautiful thing He's ever seen in His life. I may not have a clear face, or even have the cutest nails, but through God, I've got the biggest smile and I'm as perfect as can be. So no lies, no lies am I going to hear. No lies, no lies, you can tell me. I'm not ugly or friendless, because God is my friend. Oh, God is my friend.[8]

NOTES

1.   Mathieu Kerekou, Quotesea, http://www.quotesea.com/quotes/with/Kingdom+of+God (accessed 4/2/10).

2.   Charles Finney, *Revivals of Religion* (Grand Rapids, MI: Fleming H. Revell Company, n.d.), 184.

3.   Roland Allen, *The Spontaneous Expansion of the Church* (London: World Dominion Press, 1960), 94.

4.   Ibid. 54.

5.   Ibid., 102.

6.   Keith Morrison, "Face Value," *Dateline* (NBC News, 2004), http://www.msnbc.msn.com/id/3917414/ (accessed 4/13/10).

7.   Ibid.

8.   Jamie Harrison Vaughn, 2008.

Chapter Notes

Chapter 5

The Battle of the Ages

Why here is the most radical proposal ever presented to the mind of man,
the proposal to replace the present world order with God's order,
the Kingdom of God.
—H. G. WELLS[1]

The kingdom of the world has become the kingdom of our Lord
and of his Messiah, and he will reign for ever and ever.
—REVELATION 11:15

The movie *The Matrix* is about a computer hacker who learns that his entire life has been a virtual dream, orchestrated by a strange class of computer overlords in the far future. He joins a resistance movement to free humanity from lives of computerized brainwashing.[2] At one point in the movie, the hacker discovers the true reality:

> The Matrix is a system, Neo. That system is our enemy. But when you're inside, you look around. What do you see? Business men, teachers,

lawyers, carpenters. The very minds of the people we are trying to save … You have to understand, most of these people are not ready to be unplugged. And many of them are so inert, so hopelessly dependent on the system that they will fight to protect it … The Matrix is everywhere. It is all around us, even now in this very room. You can see it when you look out your window or when you turn on your television. You can feel it when you go to work, when you go to church, when you pay your taxes. It is the world that has been pulled over your eyes to blind you from the truth.[3]

This science fiction story may be entertaining, but there is a tragic truth found in it. Today, we are living in a *Matrix*-type kingdom that is giving us a false sense of reality. Unfortunately, most appear unwilling or incapable of understanding the full extent of their danger. "The god of this age has blinded the minds of unbelievers, so that they cannot see the light of the gospel of the glory of Christ, who is the image of God" (2 Cor. 4:4).

A War Few See

The Bible says that Christians are to be a light set upon a hill (see Matt. 5:14). Regrettably, like the young disciples, Christians' cultural perceptions often blind them. Many think they understand what Christianity is all about, but they sorely lack the spiritual comprehension that Jesus demonstrated and taught. He saw things a certain way, but the disciples had great difficulty adopting the same spiritual discernment.

Years ago, I heard a loud crash outside our ministry staff house in Los Banos, California. We ran out and witnessed a tragic scene. The driver of a full-size van had crashed into a young man driving a motorcycle. The older man driving the van was hysterical because the victim was an employee in his company. The motorcyclist was lying on his side in the middle of the street. I ran to him and began to pray. His body was twitching, and blood flowed from his mouth like a faucet. Later, I heard he had suffered a broken neck. Soon the medics arrived and took his lifeless body away. A few minutes later, a fire truck came and hosed down the blood that had turned the street dark red. I remember the gush of water and blood hitting the curb on its way to the nearest drainage gutter.

Ironically, within minutes of the firefighters leaving, mothers and their children began to arrive and congregate on the sides of the street. That day a parade was scheduled, and soon the musical bands, colorful floats, and happy clowns were entertaining the families sitting along the very spot where the blood had just flowed. I thought, *They don't understand what's just happened. They do not see the whole picture. They think they know what's going on but they don't.*

THE BATTLE ROYAL

Throughout Jesus' earthly ministry, something was happening that everyone else continually missed or misunderstood. There was an intense and constant battle between two perspectives of life. "This is the verdict: Light has come into the world, but people loved darkness instead of light because their deeds were evil. Everyone who does evil hates the light, and will not come into the light for fear that their deeds will be exposed" (John 3:19–20). Jesus' frequent and deliberate attacks on the prevailing kingdom were often lost in the miracles and His anointed teaching.

He was determined to penetrate this kingdom and replace it with a superior Kingdom. This was a primary focus of His ministry. These challenges are extremely important for us to recognize. It is not enough to know the values of God's Kingdom. We need to have a broader understanding of why Jesus acted the way He did and what He was trying to accomplish. This will give us a clearer sense of our calling as His followers. To help clarify, let us look more closely at the four previously mentioned values of Babylon to understand Jesus' broader agenda. His confrontation with these values reveals a direct penetration of one kingdom and replacement of it with another Kingdom.

> People were bringing little children to Jesus for him to place his hands on them, but the disciples rebuked them. When Jesus saw this, he was indignant. He said to them, "Let the little children come to me, and do not hinder them, for the kingdom of God belongs to such as these. Truly I tell you, anyone who will not receive the kingdom of God like a little child will never enter it." And he took the children in his arms, placed his hands on them and blessed them (Mark 10:13–16).

On this occasion, the parents had gone to an itinerant holy man hoping He would bless their kids. Sadly, the disciples considered children less valuable than the adult followers and potential religious leaders they wanted to influence. They were seeing the situation from a Babylonian value bias. However, Jesus saw things from a Kingdom of God perspective. As a result, He reached out to bless the children and had a strong message for the rest. He rebuked them for connecting people's value with their age. He directly confronted a kingdom that embraced this lie.

You see, Jesus was not just blessing the children. There was something more going on here. He was also intentionally tearing down a dangerous and entrenched mindset. In His Kingdom, age was irrelevant. This value was part of an old wineskin that could not hold the new wine of His Kingdom. It had to be replaced.

> A large crowd followed and pressed around him. And a woman was there who had been subject to bleeding for twelve years. She had suffered a great deal under the care of many doctors and had spent all she had, yet instead of getting better she grew worse. When she heard about Jesus, she came up behind him in the crowd and touched his cloak, because she thought, "If I just touch his clothes, I will be healed." Immediately her bleeding stopped and she felt in her body that she was freed from her suffering. At once Jesus realized that power had gone out from him. He turned around in the crowd and asked, "Who touched my clothes?" "You see the people crowding against you," his disciples answered, "and yet you can ask, 'Who touched me?'" But Jesus kept looking around to see who had done it. Then the woman, knowing what had happened to her, came and fell at his feet and, trembling with fear, told him the whole truth. He said to her, "Daughter, your faith has healed you. Go in peace and be freed from your suffering" (Mark 5:24–34).

Here was a woman who had exhausted all her money to receive treatment for her medical condition. She put all her trust in the hands of knowledgeable doctors, but they were unsuccessful. In her desperation, she sought help from someone offering hope for both body and soul. Jesus could have allowed her healing to be completely private. Instead, He called attention to the fact that someone had touched Him and healing power had gone out of Him.

I believe Jesus was making a critical point regarding the opposing kingdom values. He was signifying that His Kingdom was more powerful than the one that relied strictly on human knowledge. The Kingdom of God had healed a desperate woman where the other kingdom had miserably failed. This was a major reason why Jesus healed people. He was demonstrating the superiority of His Kingdom over one that relied too much on human intelligence. God was not against the medical profession; He was against a reliance on human knowledge that exceeded a trust in Him. Only His Kingdom had the power to raise up the hopelessly disabled, heal the incurably sick, and bring the dead back to life. Praise God!

> On reaching Jerusalem, Jesus entered the temple courts and began driving out those who were buying and selling there. He overturned the tables of the money changers and the benches of those selling doves and would not allow anyone to carry merchandise through the temple courts. And as he taught them, he said, "Is it not written: 'My house will be called a house of prayer for all nations'? But you have made it 'a den of robbers'" (Mark 11:15–17).

Jesus had entered Jerusalem one last time, knowing it would cost His life. When He reached the temple, He drove the businesses out and refused to allow anyone to carry merchandise through the temple courts. This hostile takeover began early in the week and continued for a couple of days. Never again, while He was alive, would another kingdom control the entrance to the temple.

Perhaps this incident in Jerusalem inspired the scene in the *Lord of the Rings* where Gandalf confronted the dragon-like creature called the Balrog. You might recall on the thin bridge of Khazad-dûm that connected two worlds, Gandalf shouted to the Balrog with passionate authority, "You shall not pass!" Jesus, with divine authority, was taking a similar stand but against an entire misguided culture.

From the beginning of His ministry to the end, Jesus challenged the money-loving kingdom of Babylon that wanted to dominate a Kingdom focused on spiritual riches. This issue stirred up His righteous indignation more than anything. He was angry that it dared to encroach upon the very entrance of the temple. He saw beyond the animals in their home-made cages and the hucksters with their leather moneybags. He was courageously attacking a kingdom that was obsessed with money and material riches, because in His Kingdom, earthly riches do not determine a person's value.

One of the most dramatic spiritual encounters ever recorded in Scripture was when Jesus reached out to a man possessed with a multitude of demons. This man called himself Legion and would run around naked, living in tombs of a local cemetery, frustrating every effort to capture him. The Scriptures tell us, "Night and day among the tombs and in the hills he would cry out and cut himself with stones" (Mark 5:5). His mannerisms were bizarre, his strength was spectacular, and his appearance was frightening. This meant nothing to Jesus. He reached out to the most unlovely person in the region and set him free. "When they came to Jesus, they found the man from whom the demons had gone out, sitting at Jesus' feet, dressed and in his right mind ..." (Luke 8:35).

With this miracle Jesus was sending a message, first to the local folks and then to the rest of the world. All are welcome in the Kingdom of God—even those most physically and emotionally undesirable. Physical beauty is unnecessary to be a part of Jesus' Kingdom. There is no prejudice or partiality with Him. If we are to be a part of this Kingdom, then our values will have to come into alignment with His.

THE KINGDOM MANDATE

As Jesus neared the end of His earthly ministry, He lamented the lack of receptivity to the gospel of the Kingdom. He knew tough times were ahead and that Israel was unprepared to face these trials. Christ also carried the burden of immature disciples who were constantly focusing on who was the greatest among them and the political status of their nation. In Luke 21, they demonstrated their ignorance by attempting to impress Jesus with the beauty of their religious buildings. Once more, Jesus tried to shift their focus from Babylon's values to the Kingdom of God, "As for what you see here, the time will come when not one stone will be left on another; every one of them will be thrown down" (Luke 21:6). The time for Christ's departure was imminent, but no one seemed ready. There had been only one other person who understood the battle of the kingdoms, and his head was no longer on his shoulders.

At the Last Supper, Jesus made many memorable statements. Tragically, the spiritual ineptness of His listeners was able to match the power of these final words. In the Upper Room, He declared, "I appoint unto you a *kingdom*, as my Father hath appointed unto me" (Luke 22:29 KJV). Jesus had been the embodiment of the Kingdom of God when He walked this earth. That is what made Him so radical. With His departure, He was now appointing the Church to be the visible representation of the Kingdom of God! Jesus was giving them an incredible mandate, but they missed it. If it was going to happen, they were going to need significant help.

PENTECOST OR BUST

"And he said to them, 'Truly I tell you, some who are standing here will not taste death before they see that the kingdom of God has come with power'" (Mark 9:1). Jesus was preparing them for Pentecost. Everything would change after this encounter with the Holy Spirit. In the final days of Jesus' earthly ministry, He spoke of a need to modify their preparations. "'When I sent you without purse, bag or sandals, did you lack anything?' 'Nothing,' they answered. He said to them, 'But now if you have a purse, take it, and also a bag; and if you don't have a sword, sell your cloak and buy one ...' The disciples said, 'See, Lord, here are two swords.' 'That's enough!' he replied" (Luke 22:35–36, 38).

I believe Christ's utmost concern was the potential failure of His disciples to reach Pentecost. Jesus prayed, "Holy Father, protect them by the power of your name, the name you gave me, so that they may be one as we are one. While I was with them, I protected them and kept them safe by that name you gave me ..." (John 17:11–12). He knew the truths of the Kingdom would become abundantly clear at Pentecost, but they would face many dangers, fears, and confusion before then. They might even have to defend their lives. Pentecost and the subsequent baptism of the Holy Spirit was the empowerment the young Church desperately needed to live and expand the Kingdom of God.

One of the disciples' most vulnerable moments came when the soldiers arrested Jesus in the garden of Gethsemane. Presumptuous Peter wielded his sword, but Christ demonstrated He was all the protection and care they needed. It is very significant that Jesus would not allow the soldiers to arrest Him until they first agreed to let the disciples leave safely (see John 18:4–9). Their survival was His greatest concern.

THE BATTLE BEYOND THE GRAVE

This conflict between two kingdoms raged throughout Christ's ministry and followed Him all the way from the manger to the cross. Throughout His life, Jesus miraculously escaped every attempt upon His life. However, this supernatural ability faced the ultimate test when, as an unwarranted prisoner, He stood bound before Pontius Pilate. Jesus faced an unprecedented threat from the combined religious, political, and military forces. With no help in sight, amazingly, Pilate's wife experienced a deeply disturbing dream the night before. As a result, she sent a message to Pilate telling him to leave Jesus alone.

This again was Jesus' miraculous way of escape. However, this time He took a different position. Rather than fleeing to Egypt or slipping through an angry mob, Jesus chose to do nothing. Even when Pilate encouraged Him to respond to the charges, Jesus remained silent. His decision to forfeit His way of escape sealed His fate. Jesus possessed a divinely directed life, and no other kingdom could take it from Him; only He could give it up. Jesus was willing to give up His life only because He knew His sacrifice would strengthen the Kingdom of God and weaken the power of all other kingdoms. This was a major focus for His entire three and half years of ministry.

When Pilate turned Jesus over to the soldiers, they proceeded to dress Him up as a king and ridicule Him. They knelt before Jesus and mockingly declared, "Hail, king of the Jews." They then took His symbolic rod of authority and struck Jesus on the head over and over again (see Matt. 27:28–30). Later, when Jesus hung on the cross, He had to endure additional mocking of His kingship by soldiers, religious leaders, robbers, and common people passing by (see Matt. 27:29–44). The entire scene reflected an epic clash of kingdoms and who was the legitimate king.

"Jesus of Nazareth, the king of the Jews" was the written message above the crown of thorns piercing His noble head (see John 19:19). What was the purpose of the sign? Was Pilate making a magnanimous tribute over the objections of the chief priests, or was it a form of mockery to add to the ceaseless barrage of painful ridicules and brutal scorn? Actually, the sign was a charge or accusation against Him. The sign declared the reason and cause of His death. He died because He dared to replace the current kingdom with His own.

This hollow sense of victory, we know, lasted only a short time. Another scene soon eclipsed the one at Golgotha—that of an earth-shaking angel casting aside a useless stone that vainly attempted to restrain the King of kings. It is a scene of a seraph, clothed in brilliance, mockingly sitting upon this pathetic rock lying prostrate at the foot of an empty tomb while nearby guards shook with fear and became like dead men. The angel understood this battle of the ages and that the Kingdom of God had just begun to fight.

PRAYER

Lord Jesus, thank You for Your furious love and courage. You never compromised for the sake of man's approval or personal comfort. You always lived and operated by the values of a higher Kingdom. Your love was never weak but proved stronger than death. You absorbed all the punishment this world and the devil could rally against You, and when the smoke cleared, You were still standing. Give me Your power and grace to do the same. In Your precious name, Amen.

NOTES

1.   E. Stanley Jones, *The Unshakable Kingdom and the Unchanging Person* (New York: Abingdon Press, 1972), 11.

2.   *The Matrix* (1999), http://www.pokergently.com/?p=218 (accessed 1/4/10).

3.   *The Matrix*: les scripts, http://www.thematrixfr.com/m1_script_vo.shtml (accessed 1/4/10).

Chapter Notes

Chapter 6

THE FIGHT IS JOINED

Give me one hundred preachers who fear nothing but sin and desire nothing but God, and I care not whether they be clergymen or laymen, they alone will shake the gates of Hell and set up the kingdom of Heaven upon Earth.

—JOHN WESLEY[1]

I will give you the keys of the kingdom of heaven ...

—MATTHEW 16:19

With a fiery intensity, Jesus had penetrated the cold religious system of His day. He courageously fought against the pleasure-loving culture of the prevailing ruling powers. With equal zeal, He reached out to the disenfranchised with a gentle heart and hand. He embraced the poor and hurting with healing and compassion. His life had successfully demonstrated the power and love of the Kingdom. Now it was time to pass the baton. Ten days after Christ's ascension, the disciples were once again in an upper room, quite possibly the same one where Christ bestowed the Kingdom upon them. They were alone this time but hopeful that the promised help would come soon. They did not have to wait long.

It is important to realize that when the Holy Spirit first came upon Jesus at the Jordan River, He came in the form of a dove. I believe this was because there was nothing amiss in Jesus' life. His mind and heart were in complete alignment with the Kingdom of God. On the other hand, when the anticipated Holy Spirit came upon the disciples on the day of Pentecost, He came as a mighty rushing wind. But why a violent tempest blast rather than a gentle resting? I believe it was because the Holy Spirit had to penetrate and replace the Babylonian values buried deep within their minds and hearts. If not successfully accomplished, they would not be able to fulfill their spiritual destiny. Only after the wind accomplished its purpose did the fire fall.

The disciples now possessed unprecedented insight and power. When Peter spoke to the thousands that had gathered, he revealed a powerfully new perception and understanding. The Holy Spirit had replaced his worldview and filled him with a powerful message. "'Get out while you can; *get out of this sick and stupid culture!*' That day about three thousand took him at his word, were baptized and were signed up ..." (Acts 2:40–41 MSG). Peter expressed the spiritual understanding the disciples had tragically lacked when they were with Jesus. With this fresh revelation and anointing, they were finally empowered to expand the Kingdom of God throughout the earth.

THE SOWER AND THE SEED

Matthew, Mark, and Luke describe the parable of the Sower and the Seed. Most are aware that the seed landed on different soils. What few consider is that the seed is actually the message of the Kingdom (see Matt. 13:19). Jesus was using the example of a farmer sowing seeds to describe how the Kingdom functions. Seeds penetrate and replace soil in a similar manner to light and wind, but seeds have another powerful characteristic—they grow and multiply.

Those three thousand new believers may have lacked knowledge and experience but it did not matter because what they had would grow. "The kingdom of heaven is like a mustard seed, which a man took and planted in his field. Though it is the smallest of all seeds, yet when it grows, it is the largest of garden plants and becomes a tree, so that the birds of the air come and perch in its branches" (Matt. 13:31–32). The greatness of their spiritual purpose was already in the womb of their little seed.

Those saved on Pentecost may have not known where to sow their seed, but Jesus said the farmer sowed it as he went out. It is safe to assume it was not far from where the farmer lived. Peter did not encourage the new believers to leave their jobs and join his ministry team. This was because he wanted them to go back from where they came and penetrate their communities with the message of God's Kingdom.

Most new seeds begin to grow when they are placed in dirt. Dirt is often composed of dead and decaying debris and is not very valuable. However, it is an excellent location to plant the Kingdom—in worthless places filled with dirty minds and lifeless hearts. The places where life was lacking was about to be penetrated by God's glorious Kingdom.

This is the true principle of sowing and reaping. They were to go and sow the Kingdom of God into their homes, city, and country. Their radical testimony, coupled with vibrant worship and prayer, reinforced by revelation knowledge of God's truth, was about to penetrate the world and replace it with life.

LIFE REDEFINED

The message Peter gave that day had come with crashing clarity from the Holy Spirit and reflected a newfound understanding of Christ's teaching on two opposing ways of living. "Enter through the narrow gate. For wide is the gate and broad is the road that leads to destruction, and many enter through it. But small is the gate and narrow the road that leads to life, and only a few find it" (Matt. 7:13–14). The word "few" means puny.[2] In other words, a very small number of people find that path to God and walk upon it. This is in contrast to the statements made at almost every funeral, "He's in a better place now." The Bible clearly tells us that most people are not on the road to life. It is of utmost importance that we evaluate what road we are on before it is too late: "Take note of the highway, the road that you take ..." (Jer. 31:21).

The two roads Christ described involved something broader than repentance from sin. Peter understood this after Pentecost and exhorted the people to disengage from a culture dominated by the ways of a fallen kingdom. He had plenty of Old Testament passages to reinforce that humanity's problem was not only *sin* but also a broader wrong *way* of living.

- "We all, like sheep, have gone astray, each of us has turned to our own *way*..." (Isa. 53:6).

- "There is a *way* that appears to be right, but in the end it leads to death" (Prov. 16:25).

- "Let the wicked forsake their *ways* and the unrighteous their thoughts. Let them turn to the Lord, and he will have mercy on them, and to our God, for he will freely pardon" (Isa. 55:7).

- "If my people, who are called by my name, will humble themselves and pray and seek my face and turn from their wicked *ways*, then will I hear from heaven and will forgive their sin and will heal their land" (2 Chron. 7:14).

The apostle Paul also described this important transition of our ways. "As for you, you were dead in your transgressions and sins, in which you used to live when you followed the *ways of this world* and of the ruler of the kingdom of the air, the spirit who is now at work in those who are disobedient" (Eph. 2:1–2).

Unfortunately, many have given their lives to Jesus but have not changed their mindsets or the way they live their lives. They have repented of immorality but have continued to view lustful images on television and movie screens. They confess sinful lifestyles but remain committed to ungodly relationships. They have allowed the truth of God's Kingdom to penetrate their lives but have not allowed it to replace anything in their hearts.

When Jesus raised Lazarus from the dead, He immediately commanded that Lazarus' grave clothes be removed (see John 11:44). Imagine the foolishness of Lazarus trying to go back to work while dressed in his grave clothes. It is not enough to rise from the dead. We need to separate ourselves from whatever has wrapped up our minds and hearts and reflects our former condition.

Paul admonished the Church in Rome, "Do not conform to the *pattern of this world*, but be transformed by the *renewing of your mind ...*" (Rom. 12:2). To be citizens of God's Kingdom, it is imperative that we have our perspective of life changed. Repentance involves more than just turning from sin; it literally means a change of thinking.

THE ETHOS OF THE KINGDOM

This change of perspective is essential to expanding God's Kingdom. In anthropology, great care is given to understand a particular culture. Often field workers will conduct a yearlong ethnographic study to learn the ways of a particular people group. They look for patterns of behavior and carefully research why such patterns might exist. They live in the same houses and eat the same food in an effort to identify and understand the culture as much as possible. They become participant observers.[3] Often they are interested in the less-tangible ethos or the fundamental values of the culture.

I believe we must have the same attitude with the Kingdom of God. Rather than focusing just on the culture of the local church, we need to study the ethos of the Kingdom. Why does the Kingdom of God operate in such a way? What is it trying to accomplish? What are its values and priorities? What are its ways?

The ways of the Kingdom appear throughout the Scriptures. They are found in the manner in which Jehovah led the Children of Israel in the Old Testament. They are revealed in the Ten Commandments, the Sermon on the Mount, and Romans 12. They are clearly demonstrated in the way Christ lived because He is inseparable from the Kingdom.

In Isaiah 55:8–9, we have an often-quoted Scripture. "'For my thoughts are not your thoughts, neither are *your ways my ways*,' declares the Lord. 'As the heavens are higher than the earth, so are *my ways* higher than *your ways* and my thoughts than your thoughts.'" This passage reveals more than God's magnificent being and character and our imperfections and distance from Him. I believe it reveals a deep longing He has for us to embrace His way of thinking and to live according to His ways.

God is searching for those who will seek Him and walk in His ways. Fortunately, He has found a few people who are interested in doing this.

David prayed, "Show me your ways, Lord, teach me your paths" (Ps. 25:4). Isaiah declared, "Come, let us go up to the mountain of the Lord, to the temple of the God of Jacob. He will teach us his ways, so that we may walk in his paths …" (Isa. 2:3). Kingdom-minded people will, "Start children off on the way they should go, and even when they are old they will not turn from it" (Prov. 22:6). Knowing the ways of the Kingdom will ultimately lead us to spread the ways of the Kingdom wherever we go.

The Penetrating Power of Truth

The ways of the King and His Kingdom is the truth we need to live by. "Jesus said to them, 'You are truly my disciples if you live as I tell you to, and you will know the truth, and the truth will set you free'" (John 8:31–32 TLB). After Pentecost, the disciples understood they had to *speak* the truth for it to penetrate the culture. They used truth to dismantle the seductive lies of the kingdom of Babylon and set the people free. "Then we will no longer be infants, tossed back and forth by the waves, and blown here and there by every wind of teaching and by the cunning and craftiness of people in their deceitful scheming. Instead, *speaking the truth in love*, we will grow to become in every respect the mature body of him who is the head, that is, Christ." (Eph. 4:14–15).

The apostle Paul wanted the Church to avoid discussions void of truth. "Do your best to present yourself to God as one approved, a worker who does not need to be ashamed and who correctly handles the word of truth. Avoid godless chatter, because those who indulge in it will become more and more ungodly" (2 Tim. 2:15–16).

Opposition Ahead

As the early Church preached the truth, something became clear; counterattacks from the opposing kingdom were inevitable. The spirit of Babylon may allow a certain degree of religious freedom, but only to a point. It will always react violently when its lies are exposed and its ways are threatened. For nearly a month, Paul enjoyed great freedom while evangelizing the city of Thessalonica, but opposition arose after a great multitude became followers of Christ. Their accusations were remarkably accurate: "These who have turned the world upside down have come here too" (Acts 17:6 NKJV). Later Paul enjoyed success in Ephesus without any meaningful resistance. Nevertheless, after the Church grew significantly again, it threatened the social and economic state of the city. That is when the people of the city, representing the prevailing kingdom, responded with violence (see Acts 19:20–27).

When I was much younger, I was given a popular child's project kit called Uncle Milton's Giant Ant Farm. It consisted of a couple of clear plastic panels with white sand in between. When the farm had a colony of ants, they would build an extensive network of tunnels and bridges that were clearly visible. For some odd reason, I never forgot the illustrated instruction manual that came with the ant farm. One of the important reminders said, "While ants are very friendly with one another in the same colony, they will fight with ants from another colony. So don't ever mix your ants, or you will start a war."[4] We may chuckle at the thought of ants going to war but we need to be aware of the unavoidable tension between the two kingdoms. "Take a lesson from the ants ... Learn from their ways and be wise!" (Prov. 6:6 TLB).

The early Church was committed to replacing the kingdom of Babylon with the Kingdom of God. They were not looking for religious tolerance; they were out to completely change the system. The reigning spiritual and physical powers recognized the threat to their positions and influence. They found it impossible to minimize or disregard the transforming power of the Kingdom. Their fears were well founded. Even the powerful Roman Empire eventually fell at the feet of this world-changing movement.

A PRESENT AND FUTURE CONFLICT

Today, the Kingdom values this country was founded upon have become minimized and used as a bargaining chip for peace. This is in sharp contrast with the example left us by Jesus and the first-century Church. The Bible says, "Make every effort to live in peace with everyone and to be holy ..." (Heb. 12), but this does not give us license to compromise the values of His Kingdom. Increasingly, we are seeing those who have embraced the kingdom of Babylon are vigorously opposing those committed to God's Kingdom.

I have come to bring fire on the earth, and how I wish it were already kindled! But I have a baptism to undergo, and what constraint I am under until it is completed! Do you think I came to bring peace on earth? No, I tell you, but division. From now on there will be five in one family divided against each other, three against two and two against three. They will be divided, father against son and son against father, mother against daughter and daughter against mother, mother-in-law against daughter-in-law and daughter-in-law against mother-in-law (Luke 12:49–53).

In Matthew 24:9–14, Jesus spoke of the last days and the condition of the world prior to His return. Several years ago, there was an emphasis on verse fourteen, "And this gospel of the kingdom will be preached in the whole world as a testimony to all nations, and then the end will come." This, for a time, became a trumpet call for increased missionary mobilization. As important as this is, something else must also occur before the end. I believe it is found in verse nine, "Then you will be handed over to be persecuted and put to death, and you will be *hated by all nations because of me.*" Currently some nations hate Christians and any allegiance to God's Kingdom but not all. This has yet to come. Someday it will—quite possibly in our lifetime.

Jesus warned His disciples so they would be better prepared to face the rulers of this world's system. But the disciples needed to know something else. Jesus said:

Be careful, or your hearts will be weighed down with dissipation, drunkenness and the anxieties of life, and that day will close on you suddenly like a trap. For it will come on all those who live on the face of the whole earth. Be always on the watch, and pray that you may be able to escape all that is about to happen, and that you may be able to stand before the Son of Man (Luke 21:34–36).

Jesus did not want His followers swayed by the prevailing Babylonian value system of pleasure-seeking, materialism, and physical security. This will be the prevalent attitude of people at this time.

The Church faced a hostile world when it was birthed two thousand years ago. Despite the opposition, great changes occurred because of the disciples' understanding of the evils of the prevailing culture and the power of God's Kingdom. Today, the spiritual state of the world is becoming increasingly similar to what the first-century Church encountered. In many respects, we have come full circle. As a result, we need to be looking for an equivalent or greater move of God to occur.

> After this I looked and there before me was a *great multitude* that no one could count, from every nation, tribe, people and language, standing before the throne and before the Lamb. They were wearing white robes and were holding palm branches in their hands ... Then one of the elders asked me, "These in white robes—who are they, and where did they come from?" I answered, "Sir, you know." And he said, "*These are they who have come out of the great tribulation*; they have washed their robes and made them white in the blood of the Lamb" (Rev. 7:9, 13–14).

Ultimately, Jesus will penetrate all opposing powers and hand over the Kingdom of God to His Father (see 1 Cor. 15:24). Until then, we need to accept a future filled with opposition against those who embrace the Kingdom of God. Nevertheless, we also need to remember the sufficiency of God's matchless grace.

> And though this world, with devils filled, should threaten to undo us,
> We will not fear, for God hath willed His truth to triumph through us:
> > The Prince of Darkness grim, we tremble not for him;
> > His rage we can endure, for lo, his doom is sure,
> > One little word shall fell him.

> That word above all earthly powers, no thanks to them, abideth;
> The Spirit and the gifts are ours through Him Who with us sideth:
> > Let goods and kindred go, this mortal life also;
> > The body they may kill: God's truth abideth still,
> > HIS KINGDOM IS FOREVER![5]

NOTES

1.   John Wesley, *The Quotable Christian*, http://www.pietyhilldesign.com/gcq/quotepages/missions.html (accessed 2/27/10).

2.   NT:3641 *oligos* (ol-ee'-gos); of uncertain affinity; puny (in extent, degree, number, duration or value); *Biblesoft's New Exhaustive Strong's Numbers and Con-*

cordance with *Expanded Greek-Hebrew Dictionary*. Copyright © 1994, 2003, 2006 Biblesoft, Inc. and International Bible Translators, Inc.

3. Brian A. Hoey, PhD, "What is Ethnography?," http://www.brianhoey. com/General%20Site/general_defn-ethnography.htm (accessed 11/18/10).

4. *Antwatcher's Manual* (Westlake Village, CA: Uncle Milton Industries, n.d.), 8. http://www.antfarmu.com/files/1622584/uploaded/Ant-Farm-Manual. pdf (accessed 1/4/10).

5. Martin Luther, "A Mighty Fortress" (1529), http://www.cyberhymnal. org/htm/m/i/mightyfo.htm (accessed 1/4/10).

Chapter Notes

Part Two

Exposing Babylon

Chapter 7

PIED PIPER OF PROSPERITY

*O*h Lord, won't you buy me a Mercedes Benz ?
My friends all drive Porsches, I must make amends.
—JANIS JOPLIN[1]

*I*f you start thinking to yourselves, "I did all this. And all by myself.
I'm rich. It's all mine!"—well, think again.
—DEUTERONOMY 8:17–18 (MSG)

I n 1284, a colorful minstrel came to the town of Hamelin, Germany. He was not there to entertain but to seek revenge for nonpayment of his rat extermination services. While the adult residents were in church, the Pied Piper lured 130 boys and girls away with his musical pipe. The children never returned.[2] It is a tragic tale but not as heartbreaking as one occurring these days.

Many adults today were zealous Christians at one time. When their hearts were ablaze with the love of God, they were innocent and free, but at some point, a mesmerizing tune lured them away from home. This Pied Piper had come from a land called Babylon, and his hidden intentions were evil too. In the next few chapters, we want to expose these melodious allurements. We want to take a hard look at fortune, fame, and the pursuit of pleasure.

> And the ones sown among the thorns are others who hear the Word; Then the cares *and* anxieties of the world *and* distractions of the age, and the pleasure *and* delight *and* false glamour *and* deceitfulness of riches, and the craving *and* passionate desire for other things creep in and choke *and* suffocate the Word, and it becomes fruitless (Mark 4:18–19 AMP).

Babylon is in love with money, the material goods money will buy, and the success that comes with having it all. The deceitfulness of riches can be illustrated through the story of an American investment banker and a Mexican fisherman.

THE COLLISION OF WORLDS

The American investment banker was at the pier of a small coastal Mexican village when a small boat with just one fisherman docked. Inside the small boat were several large yellow fin tuna. The American complimented the Mexican on the quality of his fish and asked how long it took to catch them.

The Mexican replied, "Only a little while."

The American then asked, "Why didn't you stay out longer and catch more fish?"

The Mexican said he had enough to support his family's immediate needs.

The American then asked, "But what do you do with the rest of your time?"

The Mexican fisherman said, "I sleep late, fish a little, play with my children, take siesta with my wife, Maria, stroll into the village each evening, where I sip wine and play guitar with my amigos. I have a full and busy life."

The American scoffed, "I am a Harvard MBA and could help you. You should spend more time fishing and with the proceeds, buy a bigger boat. With the proceeds from the bigger boat, you could buy several boats. Eventually you would have a fleet of fishing boats. Instead of selling your catch to a middleman, you would sell directly to the processor, eventually opening your own cannery. You would control the product, processing, and distribution. You would need to leave this small coastal fishing village and move to Mexico City, then LA, and eventually New York City, where you will run your expanding enterprise."

The Mexican fisherman asked, "But how long will this all take?"

The American replied, "Fifteen to twenty years."

"But what then?"

The American laughed and said, "That's the best part. When the time is right, you would announce an IPO and sell your company stock to the public and become very rich. You would make millions."

"Millions… Then what?"

The American said, "Then you would retire. Move to a small coastal fishing village where you would sleep late, fish a little, play with your kids, take siesta with your wife, stroll to the village in the evenings where you could sip wine and play your guitar with your amigos."[3]

Money is a core value in Babylon, and its citizens have become obsessed with getting as much of it as possible. Sadly, a worldwide economic system is operating nonstop to facilitate this pursuit. The great revivalist Charles Finney once noted:

> The whole system recognizes only the love of self. Go through all the ranks of business men, from the man that sells candy on the sidewalk at the corner of the street, to the greatest wholesale merchant or importer in the United States, and you will find that one maxim runs through the whole, to "buy as cheap as you can, and sell as high as you can, to look out for number one," and to do always, as far as the rules of honesty will allow, all that will advance your own interests, let what will become of the interests of others.[4]

This way of thinking has been so ingrained within us that it resists any objective analysis. All our lives, the world has operated this way. We could even point to nature to justify our "me-first" attitude. After all, isn't life based on the survival of the fittest? Who is going to look out for number one if we don't?

How we handle our finances reveals to which kingdom we belong. God wants us to make an honest living but too often, we are looking for a "me-win" rather than a "win-win" result. In chapter 16, I will share with you what this "win-win" could look like. The question is, are we focusing on enhancing just our own lives or are we also concerned about others? Do the financial resources we have belong to us or are we actually stewards of His resources?

We all know that the economic world has become very unstable. Much of this is because of selfishness. We are finding that people are increasingly willing to sacrifice their morals in an effort to expand their wallets. Jesus recognized this and was not afraid to address the problem. Out of the thirty-eight parables He gave in the Gospels, sixteen had to do with money![5] He consistently preached a message that was radically different from the prevalent culture. "No one can serve two masters. Either you will hate the one and love the other, or you will be devoted to the one and despise the other. You cannot serve both God and money" (Luke 16:13). He taught His followers to turn from the ways of the world and focus on increasing spiritual riches.

Jesus lived a simple life but He was not poor. He actually had a carpentry skill that placed Him in a respectful working-class position. He wore a finely woven robe. He did not dress or act as a beggar. He often visited the rich and powerful in their homes as well as the poor in the dirt. He was able to identify with both. Viv Grigg, a missionary to the slum dwellers of Manila, Philippines, described his social position as a "poor rich man."[6] I like that.

> Since we entered the world penniless and will leave it penniless, if we have bread on the table and shoes on our feet, that's enough. But if it's only money these leaders are after, they'll self-destruct in no time. Lust for money brings trouble and nothing but trouble. Going down that path,

some lose their footing in the faith completely and live to regret it bitterly ever after (1 Tim. 6:7–10 MSG).

ADDICTION TO STUFF

From an early age, our culture teaches us to pursue wealth to fulfill the American Dream. We face pressure to purchase a nice house with a white picket fence. As a result, many have become house poor and financially stressed. We are encouraged to buy a new car or two along with some recreational vehicles and equipment. Our garages quickly fill up with the stuff. The mantra of our culture has been, "He who dies with the most toys, wins." We are so indoctrinated that we cannot see how illogical the whole pursuit is. Even the irreverent comedian George Carlin recognized this. In one of his famous skits, he poked fun at our obsession with "stuff."

> That's all I want, that's all you need in life, is a little place for your stuff, ya know? I can see it on your table; everybody's got a little place for their stuff. This is my stuff, that's your stuff, that'll be his stuff over there. That's all you need in life, a little place for your stuff. That's all your house is: a place to keep your stuff. If you didn't have so much stuff, you wouldn't need a house. You could just walk around all the time.

> A house is just a pile of stuff with a cover on it. You can see that when you're taking off in an airplane. You look down; you see everybody's got a little pile of stuff. All the little piles of stuff. And when you leave your house, you gotta lock it up. Wouldn't want somebody to come by and take some of your stuff. They always take the good stuff. They never bother with that crap you're saving. All they want is the shiny stuff. That's what your house is, a place to keep your stuff while you go out and get … more stuff! Sometimes you gotta move, gotta get a bigger house. Why? No room for your stuff anymore.[7]

Unfortunately, many Christians and churches are following the reckless pursuit of more stuff. While the moral spotlight has been on abortion and homosexuality, the Church has overlooked the problem that is plaguing nearly every household in America. She has embraced materialism and has abandoned her mandate to establish God's Kingdom on earth. I once heard a radio preacher counsel a young woman who had called in seeking advice for finding a husband. He brashly advised her, "If he ain't got money, honey, forget it." How tragic. As long as our priorities center on physical prosperity, we cannot expect to fulfill our spiritual calling.

PATRIARCHAL PROSPERITY

Some people may object and point to the wealthy patriarchs in the Old Testament. They owned much, but God still used them. Isn't that an acceptable model for us? If we want to use Abraham as an example to justify our pursuit of money and material possessions, then we need to look a bit deeper into his life.

When faced with a famine, Abram made a strategic compromise by leaving Canaan where God had called him and going to Egypt. Once on the highway, Abram made another fateful error, hoping to secure success in his new location. With his wife, Sarai's complicity, Abram spun a tale about his marital status. Because of Abram's deception, the Egyptians gave him many material riches.

So what was so wrong with increasing wealth at the expense of the pagan Egyptians? First, in this situation, Abram was given many servants as gifts, which included a certain maidservant named Hagar (see Gen. 16:1). She would later play a key role in setting in motion ethnic conflicts that continue to this day. Second, because Abram received much livestock, his nephew, Lot, was no longer able to dwell close to him (see Gen.13:6). Without this partnership, Lot had to rely on his own limited abilities. This led him to settle outside of the city of Sodom. Soon, Lot became a victim in the battle between the king of Sodom and the king of Shinar. As a result, Lot became a captive, and Abram became embroiled in a battle that was not his own.

Because of Abram's great wealth, he failed to provide protection and oversight to Lot and his family. To make amends, Abram routed the raiding kings, restoring Lot and his family. The king of Sodom, in gratitude for his help, tried to give Abram more riches. However, Abram had obtained a much-needed change of heart and perspective. Consequently, he promised God he would not take even a thread from a sandal belonging to the king. In addition, Abram did something that was unprecedented. He gave Melchizedek, the king of Salem, a tenth of everything (see Gen.14:20). Abram was honoring God by his proper handling of his personal possessions.

VOODOO ECONOMICS

Many years later, Abraham's decedents entered the Promised Land, where they enjoyed an incredible military victory at Jericho. Confidence was running high, but soon after they were surprisingly defeated at the battle of Ai. Through the earnest prayers of Joshua and the elders of Israel, God supernaturally exposed the sin of one of the soldiers in Joshua's army. Achan confessed, "When I saw in the plunder a beautiful robe from Babylonia, two hundred shekels of silver and a bar of gold weighing fifty shekels, I coveted them and took them" (Josh. 7:21).

Achan wanted to fight for God but at the same time desired the things of Babylon. In his mind, the Babylonian robe and the gold and silver would nicely improve his personal status without hurting anyone else. Judgment came quickly to Achan for his misguided priorities. Only by purging this value of Babylon could God bless their efforts.

In another Old Testament example, Naaman was commander of the army of the king of Aram. He was a valiant soldier but had leprosy. He went to the prophet Elisha desperate for healing. After receiving his miracle, he was anxious to pay Elisha for his services. Nevertheless, Elisha refused compensation. Elisha was a prophet detached from this world's preoccupation with wealth, but Gehazi, his servant, was not. He was very attracted to Naaman's offer. Gehazi said to himself, "I will run after him and get something from him" (2 Kings 5:20). Without Elisha's knowledge or consent, Gehazi was able to obtain some of Naaman's wealth. God exposed Gehazi's treachery and struck him with the same leprosy Naaman once had. It was a painful reminder of the danger of pursuing the values of a fallen kingdom while trying to serve the Kingdom of God.

When the apostle Paul wrote to the church in Colossae, he closed with his customary greetings from his fellow workers, including a man named Demas. Later, when Paul wrote to Philemon, he once again included a greeting from Demas. However, in his last letter, Paul wrote these poignant words to Timothy, "Do your best to come to me quickly, for Demas, because *he loved this world*, has deserted me and has gone to Thessalonica …" (2 Tim. 4:9–10). We never hear of Demas again.

CHALLENGING THE SUCCESS STANDARD

One day a man asked Jesus to help him get a disputed inheritance. Jesus responded in a surprising way. Instead of showing sympathy, He chided the man for material greed (see Luke 12:13–15). Jesus knew the source of the man's frustration was his distorted perspective of prosperity. To help correct this wrong mindset, Jesus went on to share a parable to illustrate the danger of amassing material possessions. He spoke of a rich man who had a very good year. To handle his increased profits, he decided to expand his business so that he would be set up for many years to come. He could simply eat, drink, and be merry. God called this man a fool because his life was coming to an unexpected end and he had not used his riches for building God's Kingdom (see Luke 12:16–21).

Even Jesus' brothers saw His ministry through Babylon's misguided measures of success. They felt the only way to establish a Christian organization was through human promotion (i.e., speaking tours, interviews, photo ops). They felt Jesus was naïve, and so they needed to enlighten their older, out-of-step brother. "Jesus' brothers said to him, 'Leave Galilee and go to Judea, so that your disciples there may see the works you do. *No one who wants to become a public figure acts in secret. Since you are doing these things, show yourself to the world*'" (John 7:3–4). However, Jesus refused to yield to their business formula for success.

Ironically, after Pentecost, James, one of Jesus' brothers, wrote the book that bears his name. One of the main points he later conveyed was the danger of trying to manipulate certain people to gain favor and prestige. Clearly, he now embraced a different value system.

Singer/songwriter Keith Green had a profound impact on my generation. With fiery passion, he challenged the Church to greater purity. As he connected with the Christian music industry, he became increasingly suspicious of their promotion methods. He felt much of the marketing and advertising were a reflection of something other than the Kingdom of God.

He finally took a stand by declaring he would no longer allow promoters to sell tickets to hear him sing.

Keith also started producing records without a record contract with a major distribution label. Instead, he offered the records through his mailing list. His mailing list had thousands of young zealous believers who identified with Keith's countercultural passion. Furthermore, he offered these albums on a donation-only basis. He was convinced that putting a price on the products was putting a price on the gospel. Was he too radical? Did he go too far? The point is that he took a stand against the leaven that had made its way into the Christian music industry. He was living with a Kingdom of God perspective.

How Then Shall We Live?

It seems every generation has a small percentage of non-conformists in society. These individuals have taken a resistant stand against the controlling powers of the current culture. They are very sincere and committed but far away from God. As a result, they are also often angry, rebellious, and lack discipline in their lives. They have checked out of the current culture but have not embraced the Kingdom of God. Ironically, their kingdom still contains the foundational Babylonian values of independence, pride, and promiscuity.

Now consider another subculture. Have you ever been a part of a small group in a church, or perhaps a home Bible study? Do you live in a metropolitan area? If so, think back two thousand years ago and envision your small group as the only witness for the Kingdom of God in your entire city. Imagine coming together in secret to determine how you are going to penetrate and replace this vast pagan culture. These were the circumstances facing the first-century Church.

This small band refused to head for the hills and wait for their leader's return. They attacked the world's system and won. So what was the secret of their success despite such incredible odds? We all know something significant happened at Pentecost. We like to focus on the manifestations and miracles, but let us remember something very critical; after Pentecost, the disciples no longer focused on worldly success. The Holy Spirit had penetrated and replaced their minds and hearts with a passion for something more valuable and eternal. With a love for others burning in their hearts, they went forth and established a superior Kingdom in this world. Wow!

> They devoted themselves to the apostles' teaching and to the fellowship, to the breaking of bread and to prayer. Everyone was filled with awe at the many wonders and signs performed by the apostles. All the believers were together and had everything in common. They sold property and possessions to give to anyone who had need. Every day they continued to meet together in the temple courts. They broke bread in their homes and ate together with glad and sincere hearts (Acts 2:42–46).

NOTES

1. Janis Joplin "Mercedes Benz," *Pearl* (1971), http://digitaldreamdoor. nutsie.com/pages/lyrics/mercedes_benz.html (accessed 1/4/10).

2. The Lost Children of Hamlin," http://www.forteantimes.com/features/ articles/3805/the_lost_children_of_hamelin.html (accessed 11/17/10).

3. Anonymous, "The Fisherman and the Investment Banker," http://www. bluinc.com/free/fisher.htm (accessed 1/4/10).

4. Charles G. Finney, *True Saints* (Grand Rapids, MI: Kregel Publications, 1967), 95.

5. "How Many Parables Jesus Told About Money?," *Answers.com*, http:// wiki.answers.com/Q/How_many_parables_Jesus_told_about_money (accessed 1/4/10).

6. Viv Grigg, *Companion to the Poor*, (Monrovia, CA: MARC, 1990), 54.

7. George Carlin, "George Carlin on Stuff," http://www.writers-free-refer-ence.com/funny/story085.htm (accessed 1/4/10).

8. Jaeson Ma, "Session 3" (Bloomington, MN: unpublished transcript of message given at Contend Conference, 2008).

Chapter Notes

Chapter 8

REDEFINING SUCCESS

---

*V*isible success has never been the proof of Jesus or His followers.
—VANCE HAVNER[1]

*N*othing can hinder the Lord from saving, whether by many or by few.
—1 SAMUEL 14:6

In the book of Judges, we find an interesting story. It unfolds like a horror novel and then forces us to question our Western mindset of what constitutes true success. In Judges 19, we read of a Levite, his servant, and his concubine traveling a long way back home. Around nightfall, they come to an unfamiliar city named Gibeah but cannot find anywhere to stay. Finally, an older man from the city invites them in and begins to prepare a meal for all of them.

While they are eating, the men of the city come and start pounding on the old man's front door. They are demanding that the Levite join them in some gay sex. The old man refuses, but the visiting Levite gives them his concubine to help pacify their lusts. The men of the city rape her until dawn. The sexual abuse is so severe that she dies from the attack. The Levite discovers her lifeless body the next morning at the front door. Amazingly, he decides to place the corpse on his mule and travel the remaining distance to his home. When he arrives, he cuts her into twelve pieces and sends them to all the areas of Israel. This stirs up a nation and solidifies the event as one of the darkest episodes in Israel's history.

The Jewish nation responded by rallying an extensive army to fight against the city responsible for this deplorable behavior. The nation was anxious to bring justice to the situation and purge the land of sin. However, when they went against Gibeah and their broader tribe of Benjamin, something unexpected happened; they were soundly defeated. They lost twenty-two thousand men on the battlefield the first day.

Trying to remain positive, they rallied the remaining soldiers and sought the Lord earnestly. The Lord spoke to them to go against the wicked men again. What happened when they obeyed? They were defeated again. In the process, they lost an additional eighteen thousand men. The death toll had now reached forty-thousand.

They wept, fasted, and sought the Lord earnestly, and the Lord said, "Go, for tomorrow I will give them into your hands." They obeyed again, and this time they were finally victorious. They counted their slain enemies, and the total was just over twenty-five thousand.

When the fighting was finished, Israel lost fifteen thousand more men than the enemy. Now, we need to ask ourselves—was this a successful military campaign? Would a military commander use this battle as a model for a future military operation? Probably not.

The problem is that we look at this story through a Babylonian mindset of success. Our mindset would say that they were not very successful. They lost far too many soldiers. The cost was too high, and the return on investment was too low. Someone was to blame; the soldiers were not trained adequately, the generals had not planned sufficiently, or the religious leaders were getting false guidance.

But what if God does not look at this battle the same way as Babylon does? What if His position was that sin is unacceptable no matter what it costs to remove it? If that were the criteria, were they successful? What if obedience to the Word of the Lord is God's true measure of success; were they then successful? What if their victory was determined by their willingness to obey consistently; were they then successful?

This Scripture passage drew me to an important question. How do we define success? More importantly, how does God define success? Is it the house we live in, our annual income, or the type of car we drive? Alternatively, is it our commitment to moral integrity? Is it a willingness to suffer for righteousness' sake? Is it a commitment to obedience and faithfulness to the truth?

KINGDOM-SIZE SUCCESS

Does God want us to succeed in life? Of course He does. The problem is that the two opposing kingdoms differ greatly in what success is based on. The church in Corinth was prosperous materially and was probably perceived as successful. However, Paul was more concerned about their spiritual success. He used his own life to illustrate this: "Through glory and dishonor, bad report and good report; genuine, yet regarded as impostors; known, yet regarded as unknown; dying, and yet we live on; beaten, and yet not killed; sorrowful, yet always rejoicing; poor, yet making many rich; having nothing, and yet possessing everything" (2 Cor. 6:8–10).

In the book of Revelation, Jesus chided the church in Laodicea because it based its success on material prosperity rather than spiritual riches. "You say, 'I am rich; I have acquired wealth and do not need a thing.' But you do not realize that you are wretched, pitiful, poor, blind and naked" (Rev. 3:17). On the other hand, Jesus encouraged the church in Smyrna, "I know your afflictions and your poverty—yet you are rich! …" (Rev. 2:9).

What is God's real priority for our lives? Is it that we obtain the American Dream of peace, prosperity, and much property? Is it that blue and white-collar workers become prosperous according to this world's measure of success? No, it is not His priority. This might be disappointing news but I am convinced it is true. His measurements of success are completely different from this world. It is not the amount or value of our material possessions. It is not our earning power, stock portfolio, or net worth. Success in God's Kingdom is based on things of higher spiritual value.

When God does address material prosperity, it often has a spiritual connection. The Lord chose to bless Solomon when he embraced the values of God's Kingdom. Later Solomon writes, "Whoever pursues righteousness and love finds life, prosperity and honor" (Prov. 21:21). The apostle John wished material prosperity on those he cared for because he knew they had already established Kingdom values, "Beloved, I pray that in all respects you may prosper and be in good health, *just as your soul prospers*" (3 John 2 NASB).

The poor came to Jesus because they thought their problems were physical. Jesus responded to them in love but knew their primary problem was spiritual poverty. Most people have compassion for the poor and the suffering they face daily. Nevertheless, we learned in our urban ministry that we could not become so involved in relieving physical suffering that we overlook their core spiritual needs.

So Who Is Poor?

The great prophet Elisha worked with a school of younger prophets. One of these young prophets died, leaving his family in a difficult position. "The wife of a man from the company of the prophets cried out to Elisha, 'Your servant my husband is dead, and you know that he revered the Lord. But now his creditor is coming to take my two boys as his slaves.' Elisha replied to her, 'How can I help you?' …" (2 Kings 4:1–2). Here was a situation where a godly man was not only poor but also in debt. The way Elisha responded leads us to believe that he did not think the young prophet had lived anything but an honorable life. Although the family was poor and in debt, they were not defective. They also were not alone.

When Jesus addressed a large crowd of His disciples, He said, "Blessed are you who are poor, for yours is the kingdom of God" (Luke 6:20). Jesus knew that some of His disciples were paupers and beggars, and following Him was not going to change that. In addressing their condition, He encouraged them to consider the wealth they possessed in His Kingdom rather than the lack they had in this world.

Later, Jesus told the story of righteous Lazarus who was once an ailing beggar living in the shadows of riches and prosperity. His struggles continued until the day he died. Only then, did Lazarus finally enjoy health, peace, and comfort in paradise.

Many would regard Paul as the greatest apostle who ever lived. It is hard to deny the importance of his ministry in the early Church. It seems reasonable that he would enjoy a comfortable living. However, the Scriptures reveal quite the opposite life for Paul and his associates, "To this very hour we go hungry and thirsty, we are in rags, we are brutally treated, we are homeless" (1 Cor. 4:11).

Often Jesus healed the sick but did not financially restore the poor. Why? Because He did not look at the poor as deprived like we do. Rather, He focused on preaching the Good News to them (see Matt. 11:5; Luke 4:18). I believe the poor were more receptive to the Kingdom of God because they were typically less attached to the Babylonian value system (see Luke 6:20). In addition, those who lack materially often have a greater sense of their need for God. Suffering material lack fosters God-dependency, while experiencing material abundance often fosters self-sufficiency and independence. Therefore, Jesus was attracted to the poor because of their need *and* because of their natural dependency. In our urban ministry to the poor and marginalized, I became acutely aware of their physical needs, but I also became irresistibly attracted to their openness to the gospel.

In the early Church, many believers faced material hardships. One particular group was the widows. However, the Church did not assist *all* the needy widows. Strict guidelines by the Church narrowed the recipients considerably. It was not assistance based solely on a lack of material resources (see 1 Tim. 5:9–10).

James, the brother of Jesus, actually viewed the poor as being in a greater position than the rich are. "Believers in humble circumstances ought to take pride in their high position. But the rich should take pride in their humiliation—since they will pass away like a wild flower" (James 1:9–10). He further explains in James 2:5, "Has not God chosen those who are poor in the eyes of the world to be rich in faith and to inherit the kingdom he promised those who love him?" Many preach today that if we have great faith we will not be poor, but is this consistent with James' admonitions? What if we had to choose between great faith and great riches? Which would we choose?

There was a woman in Israel who gave generously to the Lord, but her husband died, leaving her with very little income. She did not stop giving to the Lord's work, although the amount was considerably less. In her impoverished state, Jesus took note and honored her. "Calling his disciples to him, Jesus said, 'Truly I tell you, this poor widow has put more into the treasury than all the others. They all gave out of their wealth; but she, out of her poverty, put in everything—all she had to live on'" (Mark 12:43–44). From a Kingdom perspective, she had given more in her poor state than she ever had in her abundance.

Poverty, therefore, is a relative term. You can be poor in the Babylonian kingdom context but rich in the Kingdom of God. Does this mean we should seek to be poor? No. Does this mean we should neglect the needs of the poor? No. Does this mean we need to adjust our thinking to a superior Kingdom of God perspective? Definitely Yes.

GIVING LIFESTYLE

In the kingdom of Babylon, the focus is on receiving, while in the Kingdom of God, giving is greater than receiving. There is no focus on maximizing personal gain at the expense of someone else. Rather, there is a focus on maximum benefit to others. John 3:16 tells us "For God so loved the world that he *gave* ..." God unselfishly gave to this world with no demand to receive reciprocally from us. This is the heart of His heart. I believe God has always had a pressure on His heart to give. It is what He *desires* to do. Those who follow Him will want to do the same. So what should be our motivation for receiving from God? Perhaps we should focus on fulfilling His desires to give rather than our desires to receive.

Churches mention giving today, but it has an unfortunate twist. We are often encouraged to give *so that* we will receive increased material benefits. Regrettably, receiving then becomes the ultimate goal rather than giving. Such church teaching on giving reflects the spirit of this world rather than the Kingdom of God. Receiving should only be a byproduct, not the prime reason for our giving. It is similar to a political candidate giving groceries to a poor single mother. It appears noble until we realize that the cameras were rolling to capture the scene for his next campaign commercial. This broader perspective reveals the candidate's true motivation; he was giving mercy so that he could receive more votes. So sad.

One day the Lord spoke simply to my heart, "Live to give." In the Kingdom of God, success is based on how much we give rather than how much we receive. The Scriptures make this clear in Acts 20:35, "It is more blessed to give than to receive." The essence of the Ten Commandments is giving honor to God and others. In Romans 13:7, we are reminded, "Give everyone what you owe them: If you owe taxes, pay taxes; if revenue, then revenue; if respect, then respect; if honor, then honor." This is a giving lifestyle.

This lifestyle needs to touch every area of our lives—even eating at restaurants. Christians are often bad tippers and leave the place a mess. This is inconsistent with His Kingdom values and a false representation of the King. We must always be ready to give. We never know who is watching our lives.

Once a rich ruler approached Jesus and asked, "What must I do to inherit eternal life?" (Luke 18:18). His question revealed a heart focused on receiving. Jesus looked at him intently and said, "You still lack one thing. Sell everything you have and give to the poor, and you will have treasure in heaven. Then come, follow me" (Luke 18:22). Jesus did not necessarily want the rich ruler to be poor. The Lord simply challenged the man to embrace an essential value in the Kingdom of God.

Shortly after, Jesus encountered another rich man. This time the result was different (see Luke 19:1–11). Zacchaeus gladly abandoned his love for money to embrace the Kingdom. He became an extravagant giver. Jesus then made the statement that "the Son of Man came to seek and to save what was lost." I believe this statement was not just in reference to Zacchaeus but all those who are lost in a materialistic, self-serving value system.

From Jesus' perspective, giving financially to the poor was helpful to the recipients but *more helpful to the donors*. This act of giving helped establish this Kingdom value in the donors' hearts. "Do not store up for yourselves treasures on earth, where moths and vermin destroy, and where thieves break in and steal. But store up for yourselves treasures in heaven, where moths and vermin do not destroy, and where thieves do not break in and steal. For where your treasure is, there your heart will be also" (Matt. 6:19–21).

Another parable of a shrewd manager illustrates the importance of using our earthly wealth to further the Kingdom of God. "I tell you, use worldly wealth to gain friends for yourselves, so that when it is gone, you will be welcomed into eternal dwellings" (Luke 16:9). The reward of using our finances for His Kingdom is seeing people meet Christ and live with Him forever. Someday these people will welcome us with open arms and thankful hearts.

THE GIFTS THAT KEEPS ON GIVING

Giving often includes material gifts, but the Gospels also mention spiritual gifts. Jesus occasionally fed the crowds but typically focused on gifts that were spiritual in nature. Perhaps this was because He did not possess many material resources and because He knew that most of the "stuff" we give lasts only a brief time and then is forgotten.

Imagine, if you can, Joseph and Mary loading up the minivan and taking the family to Grandma's house for Christmas. Everyone wondered what little boy Jesus would give this year. What Jesus gave did not come in a pretty paper and a curly bow. Throughout His life, He gave gifts much more valuable and enduring than physical presents.

1. Jesus gave love. He blessed those who were poor in spirit, discouraged, and spiritually hungry. He blessed the meek, merciful, and peacemakers. He blessed the persecuted, the poor, and the little children.

2. Jesus gave the gift of healing and restoration for those who were physically handicapped and suffering. He made sick people whole.

3. Jesus gave His time. Even though He focused on a task that had global implications, He always had time for the individual person—especially if he or she was in need. Blind Bartimaeus, the woman at the well, and

Zacchaeus the tax collector were just a few of the many recipients of His generous gift of time.

4. Jesus gave hope, forgiveness, and restored relationships in a world filled with hopelessness, hurt, and brokenness. He was the Good Shepherd.

5. Jesus gave His life. By paying the ultimate price, He gave the ultimate gift. "Greater love has no one than this: to lay down one's life for one's friends" (John 15:13).

Going to my parents' house in northern Minnesota is a Christmas tradition for all in our family. The typical celebration includes friendly conversation, lots of food, and many presents. A recent Christmas was different. Before receiving any gifts, we all chose names out of a hat, and one after another, we prayed for the person we had selected. Tears flowed as blessings were prayed for those in our family. There was a fresh awareness of spiritual giving that eclipsed the material gifts that are too often associated with our Christmas celebration. Several commented that we had found a new and special Christmas tradition!

Prayer

Lord Jesus, give us new minds as well as new hearts. Help us to think as You do. Our minds are so full of misconceptions and false assumptions. We have made our physical prosperity the focus rather than Your Kingdom. We have been guilty of using You and Your great name to facilitate our addiction to muchness, bigness, and stuff. Forgive us for selling out Your eternal, culture-changing values for things that perish. Teach us how to be extravagant and cheerful givers so that the world will discover Your superior values. For Your Kingdom's sake, amen.

Notes

1.   Vance Havner, *The Quotable Christian*, http://www.pietyhilldesign.com/gcq/quotepages/trials.html (accessed 3/2/10).

Chapter Notes

Chapter 9

POPULARITY PEAK

*Popularity is the easiest thing in the world to gain,
and it is the hardest thing to hold.*
—WILL ROGERS[1]

For they loved human praise more than praise from God.
—JOHN 12:43

One of the great thrills I have enjoyed in my life was climbing to the summit of Mt. Rainer in Washington State. At 14,411 feet, it is one of the most challenging climbs in North America. At one point, near the top, I remember looking down and seeing the clouds far below. I then looked out to the horizon past several cloud-piercing mountain peaks in the Cascade Range. It was so high and breathtakingly beautiful that I started to faint and had to catch myself. I remember our guide telling us that only half of those who attempt to reach the peak are successful. Some have even used the mountain as training for Mt. Everest—which is twice as high!

At 29,029 feet, Mt. Everest represents the virtual top of the world, and to climb it is an incredible accomplishment. Over two thousand people have reached the peak, but over two hundred have died in the attempt.[2] Every climber faces incredible dangers of wind, rock, and ice. However, the most critical challenge is coping with the oxygen levels that decrease with each ascending step. Beginning around twenty-six thousand feet, climbers enter the infamous "Death Zone." Typically, climbers can only endure the Death Zone for two to three days. At this altitude, most people lose all ability to acclimate to the low oxygen levels. Their bodies begin to deteriorate and die. If they do not descend, they could experience High Altitude Cerebral Edema (HACE). This life-threatening condition is the result of swelling in the brain from fluid leakage. An outstanding physical achievement can quickly turn into a life-threatening situation if they try to stay too long.

THE PRICE OF POPULARITY

People have made incredible sacrifices to reach the top of our highest mountains. People have also made great efforts to reach the peaks in business, sports, and politics. Some want to go beyond stardom and obtain superstar status. They want a permanent place in the clouds. In an effort to maintain their position and popularity, they have created a golden cage—a never-ending preoccupation with maintaining their position. They must hire others to help them keep on top. They try to fight off other challengers to their throne. Corporate earnings, reviews, and opinion polls often consume their lives. This is an environment plagued with pride, suspicion, and jealousy.

In the world of politics, elected officials have occasionally engaged in various unethical or illegal activities. Typically, the press jumps on the story. They investigate the reports and seek comments from the accused. A typical response is, "These charges are baseless. They are politically motivated, and I will not step down." The people accused resist vehemently any effort to bring them down. What they fail to realize is their obstinate effort to maintain their position will often kill their careers. Most people believe that if leaders have been corrupt, if they have failed the public trust, and if they have been found derelict in their duties, they need to come down.

This is to protect others from the consequences of their actions and to keep them from influencing others to repeat their mistakes.

Today there is a crisis in the Church. Corruption, immorality, and pride have infected some of the largest ministries in America. The press has exposed many Christian leaders in their hypocrisy and sin. Sadly, in an effort to remain in power, these fallen leaders have often blamed Satan, the government, or competitive ministries. Several have eventually lost their churches and brought many down with them. In the midst of these tragedies, it seems no one is talking about how the Kingdom of God operates.

Currently, many good Christian leaders and ministries are in elevated positions in the Body of Christ. There is nothing inherently wrong with this. In most cases, they are there because God put them there. However, this position comes with a warning label—the higher you go, the more you run the risk of staying on top too long. If they do not come down for a time, sin will creep in, resulting in tremendous loss. In the Kingdom of God, there is great value in coming down as well as going up. The biblical account of the Transfiguration illustrates this.

JUDICIOUS DESCENT

One day, Jesus and three of His closest disciples climbed a mountain. At the summit, Jesus' face and clothes became brilliant. Soon Moses and Elijah appeared and talked to Him. The disciples were overwhelmed with the experience, especially Peter. He managed to blurt out, "Master, it is good for us to be here. Let us put up three shelters—one for you, one for Moses and one for Elijah ..." (Luke 9:33).

Peter was trying to extend their stay, but Jesus knew something the disciples failed to realize—He knew the danger of them staying too long. They were not above twenty-six thousand feet, but the disciples were facing the same deterioration in the spiritual realm. Prolonged exposure would likely lead to spiritual pride (swelling of the brain) and an overinflated view of their abilities. They had to return to the base of the mountain in order to survive. They had not yet exhibited the symptoms of altitude sickness. There was no sin here but a necessary preventative step.

THOSE WHO REFUSE TO COME DOWN

Saul was the first king of Israel. Prior to obtaining his position, the well-respected prophet, Samuel, visited him. On this visit, Samuel invited Saul for dinner. This prompted Saul to inquire about the extraordinary favor he was experiencing, "Saul answered, 'But am I not a Benjamite, from the smallest tribe of Israel, and is not my clan the least of all the clans of the tribe of Benjamin? Why do you say such a thing to me?'" (1 Sam. 9:21). In other words, Saul did not think he deserved this type of honor. God, though, had an incredible destiny for this insignificant and humble man. When Samuel anointed Saul king, it set in motion a change of heart and increased spiritual power. Shortly after, the Spirit of God fell upon Saul, giving him zeal and courage to lead the nation of Israel into battle.

Regrettably, something tragic happened along the way. Saul lost the values that originally made him attractive to God. He became self-sufficient, arrogant, and presumptuous. As God's Spirit began to lift off him, he became cowardly and jealous. We all know the stories of his attempts on David's life, but what we often miss is the reason behind his jealousy and fear. The Scriptures tell us he was obsessed with his family maintaining the throne. Saul told his son, Jonathan, "As long as the son of Jesse lives on this earth, *neither you nor your kingdom will be established ...*" (1 Sam. 20:31). This was the root problem—Saul wanted his family to stay on top.

The book of Jeremiah records the frustrating relationship between the prophet Jeremiah and Zedekiah, the king of Judah. The Lord, through Jeremiah, repeatedly warned King Zedekiah to accept the fact that his reign was ending. But the king refused to accept this prophecy. Jeremiah further warned that great personal harm would come to Zedekiah if he did not submit to the invading king. Again, he did not listen. When Zedekiah tried to escape the siege on Jerusalem, he suffered a terrible fate; his sons were slaughtered before him, and his captors put out his eyes and threw him into prison for the rest of his life. Three times in Scripture this tragic story was repeated to serve as a vivid reminder of the importance of coming down when the Lord directs (see 2 Kings 25:4-7; Jer. 39:1–7; 52:6–11).

Several years ago, a story broke of a very popular and talented television evangelist living a double life. He publicly and tearfully confessed his sin. There remained some skeptics, but many people were happy to see signs of true brokenness. The focus began to shift to the restoration process he would go through. He was a member of a large denomination, so his submission to denominational leaders was going to be a key component. Those in authority investigated the charges and the evangelist's response. Finally, they gave their ruling—a one-year suspension from the ministry. Sadly, the evangelist refused to accept the ruling. He felt it would ruin his popular ministry, and he refused to step down. He did not want to come down the mountain. Today this evangelist's ministry is but a shell of its former glory. He never was able to regain public confidence and trust.

MINISTRY MADNESS

Sorry to say, this story is not an isolated exception. Several leaders, raised up by God, miss the fact that they may have to come down from their elevated positions. Tragically, to them, coming down is worse than death. They do not understand that the more they resist coming down, the more dangerous their position becomes. If they agree to come down, they have a much better chance of rising again.

Today, like every generation, God is looking for those whose hearts are set toward Him. He often blesses some simple, obscure, unknown person with fresh love and revelation. These individuals have a newfound desire and power to share with others. Dramatic results quickly follow. Soon meetings are set up, an organization created, and staff members are hired. A mailing list and website materialize, along with numerous supporting products.

The problem with the new ministry may be in its assumptions. Without a second thought, it presumes it should continue to exist and simply go higher and higher. Overlooked is the fact that God often gives certain revelation for a finite time or season. The ministry mistakenly assumes it is their calling and destiny to continue to grow and expand. This disconnect becomes more obvious when the ministry begins to experience a reduction in popularity and a significant financial downturn. To respond to their crisis, they increase their financial appeals and bring in consultants. Their focus has now shifted to maintaining the organization, and consequently, their program has replaced His presence.

PEACE IN THE VALLEY

After Saul's failures, God sought for a king after His own heart. He elevated the shepherd boy David through the slaying of Goliath. Soon David came to Saul's royal court, but it was not long before Saul's dogged determination to maintain the throne put David's life at risk. Miraculously, David escaped the king's hands to become the second king of Israel. David oversaw the growth and consolidation of the nation. He ruled with love and justice but ironically fell victim to a tragic rebellion engineered by his own son. David had to flee once again for his life.

As he did, a man from Saul's clan hurled insults and curses at him along with rocks and dirt. This public display of disrespect and scorn could have easily cost Shimei his life, but David would not allow anyone to touch him. "Leave him alone; let him curse, for the Lord has told him to. It may be that the Lord will look upon my misery and restore me to his covenant blessing instead of his curse today" (2 Sam. 16:11–12). Only after the death of Absalom was David able to reestablish his reign. At the end of his life, David faced another challenge by Absalom's younger brother, Adonijah, who also sought to be king. Once again, David was humbled but he escaped with his life, allowing his chosen son, Solomon, to assume the throne.

David is an example of someone who was elevated but then taken down several times during his lifetime. Unlike Saul, he accepted the ascensions and descensions as a part of his spiritual mission. Because he desired to follow God whatever the cost, David embraced the changes in direction on his personal journey.

One of the keys to the apostle Paul's success was an understanding of this spiritual dynamic. Prior to conversion, he enjoyed the elevated position of a religious Pharisee. Nevertheless, after his Damascus road experience, he lost his reputation among peers and was treated cautiously by fellow believers. During his ministry, Paul experienced incredible revelations and blessings. However, his career also included life-threatening experiences and unscheduled stays in squalid prisons. Through all these ups and downs, he humbly submitted and surrendered himself to a sovereign God. Rather than resistance, Paul embraced everything God wanted for him. "I know what it is to be in need, and I know what it is to have plenty. I have learned the secret of being content in any and every situation, whether well fed or hungry, whether living in plenty or in want. I can do all this through him who gives me strength" (Phil. 4:12–13). Paul was willing to experience the highs and lows of serving God. When imprisonment stripped him of his freedom, he continued to write—not to complain but to encourage. He embraced each circumstance as a fresh opportunity to glorify the Lord Jesus Christ.

Reverend David Wilkerson served as pastor in small churches around Scottsdale and Philipsburg, Pennsylvania, until one day he became deeply burdened with the spiritual needs of New York gang members.[3] Shortly after, he received notoriety as the founder of Teen Challenge rehabilitation centers. However, after a few years, he passed the leadership of this ministry to his brother, Don.[4] No longer was he in the headlines, until he received an incredible prophetic vision regarding the future of the United States in 1973.[5] Suddenly, he was back onto the national stage for an extended time. Then once again, he seemed to slip graciously out of the limelight, only to reemerge as a founder and pastor of Times Square Church in New York City in 1988.[6] I believe throughout his ministry career, David Wilkerson was not reinventing himself. He was merely following the ways of the Kingdom of God.

LIVE TO CLIMB AGAIN

Now, imagine a picture with three climbers on a mountain. One is at five thousand feet, one at ten thousand feet, and one at fifteen thousand feet. The question is who is leading the group? Most would say the climber at fifteen thousand feet, but the answer lies in what direction they are going. If God is directing them down, then the last shall be first (see Matt. 19:30).

On a national level, the United States has experienced years of unprecedented blessings and favor. Nevertheless, there are now clear signs of a loss of world dominance. Our military presence is unwelcome in many countries, and we have borrowed from other nations to prop up our own ailing economy. How do we respond to this new reality? Will our country try to cling to its lofty position despite clear signs of altitude sickness? Could our economic downturn actually foster a new humility, dependency, and desperation for God?

Today there is also a crisis in the American Church. Attendance numbers have plummeted amidst questions of integrity and relevancy. The media points to the failures of many of the leaders. Much of it is with justifiable ridicule and scorn. The Church has obviously lost much of its influence in the culture. In spite of this, many Christian ministries have tried to remain faithful yet also face a reduction in programs because of a drop in financial giving. Will our Christian organizations be able to see the unseen benefit of downsizing? Will they be able to shift from going higher to going deeper with God?

Millions of individual Christians have experienced extended periods of blessing—both materially and spiritually. However, many have recently experienced job losses, financial setbacks, and home foreclosures. Others are suffering from physical and mental stress. During these difficult times, we either become angry and fearful at what has been lost, or trustingly follow God so we can live to climb again.

My son Dan once shared with me this spiritual insight. "Christians often assume life is about reaching or living at the mountaintop, and without that, they will never experience God. However, I view life as living in the valley, a place where Jesus dwelt. The mountaintop is meant to recharge your battery but not meant to run it. Your relationship with God is not defined by your experiences on the mountaintop but your obedience in the valley."

Horatio G. Spafford lost his only son to scarlet fever in 1870. A year later, the Chicago fire wiped out his real estate holdings. Two years later, Horatio lost his four daughters in a tragic accident at sea. As he later crossed the location where they had drowned, the Lord inspired him to write this song.

> When peace, like a river, attendeth my way,
> When sorrows like sea billows roll;

Whatever my lot, Thou hast taught me to say,
"It is well, it is well, with my soul!"

It is well, with my soul!
It is well, with my soul!
It is well, it is well, with my soul![7]

NOTES

1. Will Rogers, *thinkexist.com*, http://thinkexist.com/quotations/popularity/ (accessed 3/2/10).

2. "How Many People Have Died on Mt. Everest?," *Answers.com*, http://wiki.answers.com/Q/How+many+people+have+died+on+the+Mt+Everest (accessed 1/4/10).

3. "David Wilkerson—Full Length Bio," *World Challenge Inc.*, http://www.worldchallenge.org/about_david_wilkerson/dw_fullbio (accessed 4/1/09).

4. Ruth Wilkerson Harris, *The Wilkerson Legacy* (Sisters, OR: VMI Publishers, 2005), 167.

5. "The Vision and Other Writings," *World Challenge Inc.*, http://www.worldchallenge.org/en/about_david_wilkerson/the_vision (accessed 1/4/10).

6. "The History of Times Square Church," *World Challenge Inc.*, http://www.worldchallenge.org/en/about_david_wilkerson/times_square_church (accessed 1/4/10).

7. Horatio Spafford, "It is Well with My Soul" (1873), http://www.biblestudycharts.com/A_Daily_Hymn.html (accessed 3/21/10).

Chapter Notes

Chapter 10

DESCENDING THE MOUNTAIN

You've been too long upon this mountain
It's time you journey to the sea.
—JASON UPTON[1]

You have stayed long enough at this mountain.
—DEUTERONOMY 1:6

I had worked in the urban core for over ten years. Our mission in the city had seen good times and bad times. Many of our experiences are in my second book, *Liberating Love*. Some of the biggest frustrations we experienced were limited finances, limited workers, and limited results. We knew God was powerful and good, but we often felt poor, weak, and ineffective. At times, it felt like our dreams of spiritual transformation in our community were slipping through our fingers, even though it seemed we were doing all the right things. I started to get tired of falling short all the time. It seemed with every fresh idea we found a new opportunity for failure. I certainly could identify with the disciple Peter, "Master, we've worked hard all night and haven't caught anything" (Luke 5:5).

The situation reminded me once again of the Uncle Milton's Giant Ant Farm manual. Another important reminder was "Be kind to your ants. If you shake your live ant habitat, or turn it upside-down, you will wreck their tunnels and bridges ... They take great pains building their little world, and if they are disturbed too much they will die."[2] I was starting to feel like the ants that had their habitat shaken too many times.

I did not experience a crisis of faith; it was more like a crisis of hope. At times, I could feel myself dying. My spirit groaned in heaviness. Life was slowly draining out of me. I was becoming increasingly desperate, and I knew my family was feeling the same. I did not know until later that God's love was graciously taking us down the mountain. Once He revealed this to us, we were all able to embrace this part of the journey rather than resist it.

A SEASON OF BARRENNESS

So how does God bring us periodically down the mountain? One way is through barrenness. I could relate to this one, and I soon discovered I was not alone. Abram was directed by God to penetrate Canaan—the land of the curse. He obeyed, but something unexpected happened. Soon after arriving, Abram faced a local famine. Can you imagine the pictures that he had to put in his first missionary newsletter—photos of arid farmland, skinny cattle, and abandoned huts. As a result, he presumptuously decided to pack up and relocate to Egypt "to live there for a while" (Gen. 12:10). We know the trip was a disaster. Ironically, his son Isaac faced his own famine (see Gen. 26:1) as well as his grandson, Jacob (see Gen. 41:54). All three generations had to face a period of barrenness in fulfilling their destiny. Rather than climbing new heights, each generation faced its own valleys of inactivity, famine, and lifelessness. As God directs our lives, there will ultimately be fruit. However, not every step will be fruitful.

God's faithfulness is from everlasting to everlasting. The Bible reveals that Abraham developed a special friendship with God. It progressed to the point where God determined to bless Abraham in an unprecedented way. God made a covenant with Abraham that contained a wonderful promise. Abraham was to father a child through his wife, Sarah. Together, they would begin a nation that would bring great blessings to the rest of the earth (see Gen. 12). Sarah displayed grace and charm to all those who visited their home. She had the qualities necessary to be a fitting mother of a nation, but there was one small problem—she was also barren.

Later in the history of Israel, we discover a godly man whose name was Elkanah. Year after year, he went up to worship and sacrifice to the Lord at Shiloh. Elkanah had two wives, Hannah and Peninnah. He faithfully cared for both and brought them with him on his pilgrimages to worship God. As much as he cared for Peninnah, the Scriptures tell us that he loved Hannah. He would often demonstrate this by giving her a double portion of the meat sacrifice. Hannah had every reason to feel special and affirmed by her husband, but she had one problem that overshadowed everything—she was barren.

There was a priest in Israel whose name was Zechariah. He was a very godly man who was married to a woman named Elizabeth. The Bible tells us that together they "were righteous in the sight of God, observing all the Lord's commands and decrees blamelessly" (Luke 1:6). They were a godly couple living exemplary lives and fulfilling a valuable service to their nation. They were the ideal couple except for one significant detail—Elizabeth was barren.

Barrenness was no small matter in the Hebrew culture. It was more than just the inability to produce an heir or continue the family name. Barrenness was considered a reproach or even a curse. Conversely, the culture considered many children to be a blessing from God. It is hard to imagine the pressure a barren woman would feel in their society. Such women were believed to be flawed or under God's judgment. Their moral integrity questioned. Others would ignore them and even openly discredit them. This made them feel like second-class citizens or worse. Barrenness carried a cultural stigma of dishonor and shame.

THE FRUIT OF BARRENNESS

When God wants to do something big, He often goes to the barren. Why? Because God's barrenness yields the fruit of humility. Barren people do not think they have it together. They know they are dependent on God. They not only allow God to bring them down, but they are also sensitive to selfishness, pride, and independence. They live according to the passage in 1 Peter 5:6, "Humble yourselves, therefore, under God's mighty hand, that he may lift you up in due time." Notice that He "may" lift you up someday. Humility can accept that.

God wanted to raise up a nation that would usher in His Kingdom. In addition, He knew this nation needed spiritual leadership, so He determined to raise up a mighty prophet. Finally, God saw the necessity of raising up a voice that would herald the coming of the world's Savior. These were three enormous tasks that were dependent on three extraordinary women—Sarah, Hannah, and Elizabeth. The fact that they were all barren gives indisputable evidence of the power and tender mercies of God.

In Isaiah 54, nearly the entire chapter is devoted to blessing the barren. God begins by declaring they will someday burst into song, but He does not stop there. He then tells them to enlarge their tents because their descendants will penetrate nations and replace desolate cities (see Isa. 54:1-3). God is determined to use the barren to effectively penetrate the kingdom of Babylon and replace it with the Kingdom of God.

Finally, Isaiah 54 states that the barren will not suffer humiliation (see Isa. 54:4). We have already discovered that barrenness yields the fruit of humility, but God has determined that they will not be humiliated. They will not live in shame and reproach. After Elizabeth became pregnant, she declared with sincere gratitude, "In these days he has shown his favor *and taken away my disgrace* among the people" (Luke 1:25).

God reinforces His love for the barren by declaring, "For your Maker is your husband ..." (Isa. 54:5). Intimacy is the reward of the barren. God will love them as a good husband loves his wife, and this love for them is everlasting. "'Though the mountains be shaken and the hills be removed, yet my unfailing love for you will not be shaken nor my covenant of peace be removed,' says the Lord, who has compassion on you" (Isa. 54:10).

A Period of Weakness

Another way God helps us down the mountain is through weakness. Weakness produces the valuable fruit of dependency. What looks like a regrettable situation can actually help us move to a better position with God. Adverse circumstances can forge a deeper reliance on Him.

Mary and Joseph felt helpless. Mary was very pregnant, and they were travelling at the time of her due date. Funds were low, and the hotels were all booked. Soon labor pains intensified. Perhaps in her weakness, Mary cried out, "Lord, this is the Christ child. I want Him born in the finest hospital or at least the best hotel in the city. Please provide something more suitable than a smelly stable and a lowly manger. Please, Lord, I'm begging You."

The apostle Paul felt acute weakness many times in his ministry. He was beaten, stoned, and shipwrecked. He spent months in dark dungeons. He struggled with a thorn in his flesh that God refused to remove. He simply assured Paul, "My grace is sufficient for you, for my power is made perfect in weakness." Paul's response was, "I will boast all the more gladly about my weaknesses, so that Christ's power may rest on me. That is why, for Christ's sake, I delight in weaknesses, in insults, in hardships, in persecutions, in difficulties. For when I am weak, then I am strong" (2 Cor. 12:9–10).

A King Finds the Key

One of the most interesting accounts in the Bible is the way God moved during the Babylonian captivity—apocalyptic visions, fiery furnace, and a hungry lions' den. These are the stories that will keep kids attentive in Sunday school. The unsuspecting recipient of two supernatural dreams was the king of Babylon, Nebuchadnezzar. Both were powerful, but the second dream was particularly fascinating (see Dan. 4:10–17).

When King Nebuchadnezzar received the dream, he was at the mountaintop. He had become extremely powerful, successful, and prominent— perhaps more than anyone else had in the world at that time. The dream described him as a tree, "Its height was enormous. The tree grew large and strong and its top touched the sky; it was visible to the ends of the earth. Its leaves were beautiful, its fruit abundant, and on it was food for all. Under it the wild animals found shelter, and the birds lived in its branches; from it every creature was fed" (Dan. 4:10–12).

The king was in a lofty position but did not know that he had also entered the death zone. The dream went on to describe what will happen. "I looked, and there before me was a holy one, a messenger coming down from heaven. He called in a loud voice: 'Cut down the tree and trim off its branches; strip off its leaves and scatter its fruit. Let the animals flee from under it and the birds from its branches'" (Dan. 4:13–14). This was a warning that Nebuchadnezzar would lose his power, influence, and authority. The dream described a stump that would remain, and after a period of time, the king would be restored if he would "acknowledge that the Most High is sovereign over the kingdoms on earth and gives them to anyone he wishes" (Dan. 4:32).

The prophet Daniel interpreted the dream and exhorted the king to turn from his sins and change his ways. Daniel was hoping this would deter the coming judgment, but the king did not listen to God's warning. In fact, twelve months later, Nebuchadnezzar commented, "Is not this the great Babylon I have built as the royal residence, by my mighty power and for the glory of my majesty?" (Dan. 4:30). The Scriptures tell us that while these words were on his lips, a voice from heaven announced the immediate fulfillment of the dream.

Soon he was acting like a wild animal and ate grass like the cattle. His hair grew out like an eagle's and his nails like the claws of a bird. Can you imagine some of the problems this created around the house? First, they had to move Dad to the backyard where there was a nicer lawn. Not too many friends came over to visit during this time. Possibly the local kids tried to get him to eat grass they would poke through the fence. They would call, "Here Nebby, here Nebby we've got something yummy for you." When he became sick once, the family didn't know if they should take him to the doctor or the veterinarian. Who can forget the family Christmas photo with everyone sitting on hay bales and dad sporting his new cowbell?

After seven periods of time (probably seven years), Nebuchadnezzar looked up to heaven, and his sanity was miraculously restored. What happened next is beautiful, "Then I praised the Most High; I honored and glorified him who lives forever. His dominion is an eternal dominion; his kingdom endures from generation to generation" (Dan. 4:34).

The proud king who refused to come down had a completely new perspective. He recognized his dependency on God rather than his own abilities. He went on to declare, "Now I, Nebuchadnezzar, praise and exalt and glorify the King of heaven, because everything he does is right and all his ways are just. And those who walk in pride he is able to humble" (Dan. 4:37). With these words, Nebuchadnezzar fades from the pages of God's Holy Book. God brought him down through weakness and taught him to trust in the Lord rather than his own strength. He now depended on the God who is able to raise up and bring down.

A Point of Crisis

The third way God brings us to a lower level is through crisis. Look at the lives of the saints in the Bible. What was their common experience? They faced obstacles beyond their natural ability to overcome. This caused them to do more than pray; they had to cry out to God. "This poor man cried, and the Lord heard him, and saved him out of all his troubles" (Ps. 34:6 KJV).

Crisis often brings forth the beautiful fruit of desperation. Desperation declares our personal abilities have failed. Desperation insists that we touch God whatever the cost. Jesus unexpectedly met one of these desperate individuals during a visit at the home of a religious leader. "Just then a woman of the village, the town harlot, having learned that Jesus was a guest in the home of the Pharisee, came with a bottle of very expensive perfume and stood at his feet, weeping, raining tears on his feet. Letting down her hair, she dried his feet, kissed them, and anointed them with the perfume ..." (Luke 7:37–38 MSG).

This was someone who was clearly desperate. She came from an awful past and knew she needed some major changes in her life. Jesus was very sensitive to her heart's desire and reached out with love and compassion. It did not matter what she had done but what she was desperate to do. This woman was clearly refusing to be overlooked. She was refusing to be presumptuous. She refused to be denied. What was the result? Jesus set her free from her sin, her past, and her shame.

In Hebrews 11:32–38, we observe numerous accounts of individuals with great faith. Their strong faith was tested and proved as they faced desperate situations. This position made them cling to only one hope. At a critical crossroads in their lives, there was no one else who could deliver; no one else was even around. There was just one person standing there with eternity in His eyes.

Moses was in a place of desperation at the shore of the Red Sea. With no boats in sight, the Egyptian army was closing in for the kill. Something needed to happen, and it needed to happen fast. At Moses' moment of crisis, there was no one to help—except his faithful God. When the Red Sea parted for the Children of Israel and they arrived safely on the other side, Moses was so thrilled and thankful that he burst into song.

In the book of Revelation, we discover the eternal rewards awaiting us. Recently, I noticed something I had never realized before. In the midst of the worship and rejoicing, there is a beautiful song clearly heard from an unusual earthly source. Surprisingly, God does not sing this wonderful song, the twenty-four elders do not sing it, and even the angels do not sing it! Only those who found God in their place of crisis and desperation sing it; it is the Song of Moses (Rev. 15:3–4).

THE HIDDEN LIFE OF A MISSIONARY

Hudson Taylor was one of the greatest missionaries of all time. A popular book reveals his spiritual secrets. In those pages, we see how he learned to go down as well as up. This was the key to his life. A critical time came early in his ministry. When he was trying to go up, God saw the wisdom of taking him down. This was essential to handle the ministry God was giving him.

> But gradually outside interest seemed to lessen, and Mr. and Mrs. Taylor found themselves with few friends, shut up to prayer and patience. At twenty-nine and twenty-four years of age it was not easy to be set aside, cut off from the work they loved and left in the backwater of that dreary street in a poor part of London. Yet, without those hidden years with all their growth and testing, how could the vision and enthusiasm of youth have been matured for the leadership that was to be?
>
> Five long, hidden years—and we should have known little of their experience but for the discovery in an old, dusty packing-case, of a

number of notebooks, small and thin, filled with Mr. Taylor's handwritten notes. One after another we came upon them among much useless rubbish, until the complete series lay before us—twelve in number, not one missing. And what a tale was unfolded as, often blinded with tears, one traced the faded record!

For these unstudied pages reveal a growing intimacy with God and dependence upon Him. Faith is here, and faithfulness down to the smallest detail. Devotion is here and self-sacrifice, leading to unremitting labor. Prayer is here, patient persevering prayer, wonderfully answered. But there is something more: there is the deep, prolonged exercise of a soul that is following hard after God. There is the gradual strengthening here, of a man called to walk by faith not by sight; the unutterable confidence of a heart cleaving to God and God alone, which pleases Him as nothing else can.[3]

In the Kingdom of God, many were willing to go up the mountain but fewer were willing to come down. Those who were did not consider this a troublesome detour but the actual King's highway. Therefore, they did not feel deprived when they suffered dishonor and did not feel proud when they were lifted up. There is an invitation to each one of us to join with the saints who have surrendered to God's ways. He is calling us to consider Christ when faced with the God-directed fluctuations of our spiritual journey.

Your attitude should be the same as that of Christ Jesus: Who, being in very nature God, did not consider equality with God something to be grasped, but made himself nothing, taking the very nature of a servant, being made in human likeness. And being found in appearance as a man, he humbled himself and became obedient to death — even death on a cross! Therefore God exalted him to the highest place and gave him the name that is above every name... (Phil. 2:5-9).

PRAYER

Lord Jesus, help me to embrace the ways of Your glorious Kingdom rather than the misguided notions of our culture. Guide my descent from the mountain of popularity and fame. Show me the value of barrenness and weakness.

Enable me to drink of the cup of obscurity. Help me to turn every crisis into an opportunity to go deeper with You.

Burn within my being the image of Your selfless life. Deliver me, Jesus, from the desires that cause me to increase while You decrease. You came not to be served but to serve. May I do likewise for the sake of Your Name and the Kingdom You rule with eternal love. Amen.

Notes

1. Jason Upton, "Burning in the Sky," *Dying Star* (2003), http://www.hitslyrics.com/j/jasonupton-lyrics-19692/burninginthesky-lyrics-895008.html (accessed 3/10/10).

2. *Antwatcher's Manual* (Westlake Village, CA: Uncle Milton Industries, n.d.), 9. http://www.antfarmu.com/files/1622584/uploaded/Ant-Farm-Manual.pdf (accessed 1/4/10).

3. Dr. and Mrs. Howard Taylor, *Hudson Taylor's Spiritual Secret* (Chicago: Moody Press 1987), 105–6.

Chapter Notes

Chapter 11

PLEASURE ISLAND

I want it all and I want it now.
—QUEEN[1]

*B*ut she who lives in pleasure is dead while she lives.
—1 TIMOTHY 5:6 (NKJV)

ost have seen the Disney cartoon classic *Pinocchio*. It is a morality tale about a wooden puppet that becomes a little boy. In one scene, Pinocchio is naively attracted to Pleasure Island, a place that promises unlimited fun and freedom. This is over the objections of his friend Jiminy, who serves as Pinocchio's conscience. "Soon Pinocchio and the other boys begin to enjoy gambling, smoking, getting drunk and destroying Pleasure Island, much to Jiminy's dismay. Then Jiminy discovers the island has a curse that transforms boys who 'make jackasses of themselves' into real donkeys, who are then sold to work in the salt mines and circuses as part of an evil racket run by The Coachman."[2]

The uncontrolled pursuit of pleasure is a pervasive feature of the kingdom of Babylon. Today, we will suffer in lines for hours to take a ride lasting a couple of minutes. We spend thousands of dollars to win a hundred-dollar jackpot. We will jeopardize job and family to fulfill some sexual fantasy. We even find pleasure in taking risks for pleasure. America is addicted to pleasure.

THE COST OF FREEDOM

The United States has long been a symbol of freedom. This has even been at the heart of our domestic and foreign policy. We want freedom to triumph over tyranny and oppression. It sounds noble, but there is a problem. In our love of freedom, we have neglected moral restraint. We have embraced freedom but have used it as a license to engage in any pleasure we can imagine. Edmund Burke, the great English statesman, once said:

> Men qualify for freedom in exact proportion to their disposition to put moral chains on their own appetites. Society cannot exist unless a controlling power is put somewhere on will and appetite, and the less of it there is within, the more there must be without. It is ordained in the eternal constitution of things, that men of intemperate minds cannot be free. Their passions forge their fetters.[3]

Our love of pleasure is not new. Solomon was an extremely gifted king. God had given him wisdom and riches beyond any man. Yet despite his power and success, he became absorbed in excessive entertainment and pleasure seeking. Solomon stated, "Everything I wanted I took—I never said no to myself. I gave in to every impulse, held back nothing. I sucked the marrow of pleasure out of every task—my reward to myself for a hard day's work!" (Eccl. 2:10 MSG). The problem was this pleasure did not secure Solomon lasting happiness and brought eventual ruin to his reign.

The famous atheist, Bertrand Russell once said, "Life is a bottle of very nasty wine."[4] This is true for many who do not know God. One of the most common characteristics of non-Christians is boredom. This is why so many are attracted to pleasure and entertainment. They have determined there is simply nothing better to do. Boredom is an indication of a lack of intimacy with God.

Time to Clean Up

When I was young, our family would occasionally visit relatives. I had cousins who were my age, and I loved playing with their toys. Eventually, my folks would announce it was time to go. Before leaving, we had to put the toys away. This was never a pleasant time, and we protested and procrastinated as long as possible.

Today, the Father is directing His followers to put their toys away because they need to get ready to leave. It is time to clean up their mess. Where they have been visiting is not their home. However, many are ignoring His instructions because they are absorbed in their current pleasures. "As it was in the days of Noah, so it will be at the coming of the Son of Man. For in the days before the flood, people were eating and drinking, marrying and giving in marriage, up to the day Noah entered the ark; and they knew nothing about what would happen until the flood came and took them all away" (Matt. 24:37–39).

Pleasure seeking may not be specifically mentioned in the Ten Commandments, but consider its influence:

1. *You shall have no other gods before me.* Pleasure and entertainment consume our hearts. We develop a passion for pleasure at the expense of loving God and others.

2. *Remember the Sabbath to keep it holy.* Many forego church and observance of God's holy day for the sake of sports and recreation.

3. *Honor your father and mother.* Video games, movies, and the pursuit of pleasure have fostered on-going tensions between parents and their kids.

4. *You shall not steal.* We are stealing from our employers through chat discussions, computer games, and visiting pornographic websites on company time.

5. *You shall not bear false witness.* We are being dishonest about pleasure-seeking activities. We are refusing to admit obsessions and addictions.

6. *You shall not covet your neighbor's wife or belongings.* We are lusting after someone's spouse and coveting his or her stuff.

THE COST OF ENTERTAINMENT

A huge part of our pleasure addiction can be seen in our insatiable appetite for entertainment. In the United States, we spend more on entertainment than we do on groceries! Entertainment is a dominant force in our culture. The troubled economy may have affected some individual pursuits, but aspects of the entertainment industry have actually grown during an economic downturn. A recent motion picture cost 500 million dollars.[5] A new football stadium cost 1.2 billion.[6] A recent baseball stadium cost 1.5 billion.[7]

Television viewing is at an all-time high. According to a recent Nielsen report, the average American viewer watches 151 hours of TV per month.[8] That amounts to over thirteen years of uninterrupted viewing by the time a person reaches sixty-five—20 percent of our lifetime! Nielsen has no means of determining if people are paying close attention to the programs or if they just have them on in the background. At best, the values of the kingdom of Babylon are constantly inundating our subconscious and dulling our spiritual sensitivity. At worst, this unreal world has so influenced us that it has become our new reality. We have been brainwashed and held captive by a fictional world that does not need God.

Worldly entertainment produces enormous loss—in time, money, relationships, and reality. It also fosters obsessive behavior. At 500 billion dollars annually in the United States,[9] the multi-faceted entertainment industry is one of largest business sectors in our nation. Each year Americans spend:

- 213 billion for sports[10] or more than twice as much as the combined giving to all religious organizations.[11]
- 75 billion for gambling[12] or more than the GDP[13] of 130 countries.[14]
- 50 billion for TV[15] or more than the defense budget of Russia.[16]
- 21 billion for video games[17] or more than the budget for NASA.[18]

- 20 billion for movies[19]

- 17 billion for recorded music[20]

- 16.5 billion for radio[21]

- 13.5 billion for pornography[22] or more than three times the budget for the United Nations.[23]

- 12 billion for amusement parks[24] or more than the GDP of seventy-five countries.[25]

- 11 billion for performing arts[26]

This does not even include the 65 billion dollars spent on recreational drugs in the U.S.[27]

DISTORTED PRIORITIES

I have been a long time fan of the Minnesota Vikings football team. They have had some good years but have never won the Super Bowl. A Viking fan knows about heartbreak and disappointment; it seems to happen every year. For several years, I would tape every game. If they won, I would keep it for future viewing. If they lost, I recorded over it. My life often became obsessed with the hope of them winning it all. I wasted many hours on viewing games, reading articles, and studying stats.

One time I purchased tickets for a home game, but our church schedule created a conflict. I remember getting up in the middle of the service to slip out the back door. As I was leaving, I heard the pastor call for me to come and lead the congregation in prayer. Immediately, I made my way back into the church to pray and then quickly slipped back out the door. I cannot remember who won that day, but I still remember my distorted sense of priorities.

Many churchgoers have postponed an opportunity to meet with God to catch a game. Church schedules are increasingly capitulating to our love of local and national sports. Anything, from the fishing opener to our kid's soccer league to Sunday football in HD can come before church. Ironically, whether our local sports team wins or loses will not make any appreciable difference in our lives, but whether we connect with God on a consistent basis will be a huge factor in the fulfillment of our spiritual destiny. I remember trying to share this problem with a pastor at a restaurant after a Sunday morning service. Unfortunately, he could not receive it because the monitors showing his favorite baseball team were constantly distracting him!

This is not exclusive to Sundays either. Christians habitually seek Pleasure Islands in their free time, vacations, and honeymoons. When tired or stressed, they look to physical entertainment to recuperate. Doesn't God offer us something better than the world? Like Esau, Christians have sold their inheritance for the sake of temporal gratification (see Gen. 25:29–34). They have sought for immediate fulfillment when they were destined for eternal riches. God, help us!

AMUSING OURSELVES TO DEATH

I remember studying about the rise and fall of the Roman Empire in school. It is remarkable how important entertainment became to the Romans. Juvenal was a famous Roman writer in the first and second century. He wrote sixteen poems that used satire to communicate the threats facing Roman society. Juvenal lamented, "The Roman citizenry had become so addicted to entertainment and pleasure that they had lost the capability of governing themselves."[28]

Regrettably, America is looking more and more like Rome in the days of Juvenal. Even with her godly heritage, America is following in the footsteps of many former civilizations. "The average age of the world's greatest civilizations from the beginning of history, has been about 200 years. During those 200 years, those nations progressed through the following sequence:

1.   from bondage to spiritual faith;

2.   from spiritual faith to great courage;

3.   from courage to liberty;

4.   from liberty to abundance;

5.   from abundance to complacency;

6.   from complacency to apathy;

7.   from apathy to dependence;

8.   from dependence back into bondage." [29]

With all the past to teach us, we should be much more prudent regarding the direction of our future. Tragically, we have lost our way, but it did not happen overnight. There were forces at work that contributed to our current condition.

> What has so degraded our ability to reason and to communicate ideas in the more than two centuries between the founding era and the present? Simply put, modern mass entertainment.
>
> Las Vegas is a city entirely devoted to the idea of entertainment, and as such proclaims the spirit of a culture in which all public discourse increasingly takes the form of entertainment. Our politics, religion, news, athletics, education and commerce have been transformed into congenial adjuncts of show business, largely without protest or even much popular notice. The result is that we are a people on the verge of amusing ourselves to death.
>
> The mandarins of mass entertainment have a revolutionary agenda, and their methods aren't hard to understand. They intend to destroy traditional Western culture, religion, and morals by using the power of the modern entertainment media. They know, and have known for decades, that sensory images are far more effective than words for mass manipulation because they have the power to elicit an involuntary response. Images force themselves on our minds whether we like it or not; it is impossible to see a violent image or an erotic picture and not react, however fleetingly...
>
> Because of its power, because of its omnipresence, and above all, because of its depravity, modern mass entertainment is one of the greatest threats to our freedom that we have ever faced. We are dangerously close to losing the ability to sustain free republican government, because so many, under the influence of the entertainment media, have largely abandoned morality and self-restraint. The newly minted age of the Internet has hastened the process, by giving virtually every home ready access to pornography, that basest of all entertainment, with its devastating influences. [30]

Two popular futuristic novels are *1984* by George Orwell and *Brave New World* by Aldous Huxley. Even though *1984* was the more popular, *Brave New World* was probably more accurate.

> What Orwell feared were those who would ban books. What Huxley feared was that there would be no reason to ban a book, for there would be no one who wanted to read one … In *1984*, Orwell added, people are controlled by inflicting pain. In *Brave New World*, they are controlled by inflicting pleasure. In short, Orwell feared that what we hate will ruin us. Huxley feared that what we love will ruin us.[31]

"[Here] on earth you have abandoned yourselves to soft (prodigal) living and to [the pleasures of] self-indulgence *and* self-gratification. You have fattened your hearts in a day of slaughter" (James 5:5 AMP).

THE ABUSE OF SEX

She was an unexpected guest at the church I attended in San Luis Potosi, Mexico. Her eyes were so empty for an eight-year-old. There should have been life inside of her but there was nothing, absolutely nothing. Life had abandoned her. She went to the bathroom several times during the church service. Her walk was awkward and labored. There was pain in her efforts.

A neighbor had brought her to the service because she knew the little girl desperately needed help. The stepfather had just raped this precious little eight-year-old a couple of days before. He was in jail, but the damage seemed irreversible. Life had left her. This is what sexual abuse does. It destroys life. Several of the church leaders gathered around her to pray for her healing. We asked God to erase the memory of the event and to restore all the devil had robbed from her. We knew God was her only hope for recovery and fulfillment of her spiritual destiny. Regrettably, her tragic story is all too common today.

The act God created as the most tender, affirming, and unselfish physical experience a man and woman were capable of enjoying has become corrupted, distorted, and selfish. God intended sex to be the gateway to life, but it has often become the back alley of personal pain and misery.

One of the most distinguishing values of Babylon is its desire for sexual pleasure without any restraints.

Today multitudes have suffered directly or indirectly from sexual abuse. Instead of giving people an experience of intimacy, sexual abuse damages people for the sake of fleeting pleasure. Sexual abuse brutally reflects the *overshadowing* control and domination of Babylon mentioned earlier. Victims are generally devastated and scarred for life. Frequently, they develop personality disorders and sexual disorientation.[32]

Many in our society want to overthrow traditional biblical boundaries for the sake of pleasure. They want sex outside of marriage to be culturally acceptable, as well as same-sex relationships and multiple partners. Some will even push for greater acceptance of using children and animals to fulfill sexual fantasies. It has become a virtual Pandora's Box of moral, emotional, and legal predicaments—a moral pandemic in a vulnerable world.

I believe sexual immorality is the greatest cause of misery in the world. Consider all the poverty that has resulted from sex outside of marriage. Most unwed mothers have struggled to raise a baby on their own—no male role model, little, if any, child support, and a constant battle to provide a living and education for their children. Single parenthood is the fast track to poverty in the world. Often these children grow up to repeat the same mistakes as their parents—a never-ending cycle of betrayal, abandonment, and pain.

Consider the millions of abortions that are the result of immorality. Tragically, it causes not only the loss of the child's life but also leaves emotional scars on the mother. Consider how many marriages tragically end because of sexual affairs. Countless families are shattered by this sin, leaving psychological scars on spouses and children that last a lifetime. Consider how many have contracted the AIDS virus because of immorality. Moreover, how many have faced a premature death because of this incurable disease?

Going a step further, consider how many are alive today that are the result of an illegitimate sexual encounter. By no fault of their own, they bear the shame of knowing they are the result of something gone wrong rather than something gone right. Sex outside of biblical boundaries creates extremely damaging consequences. Consider some of the following results.

- There have been fifty million abortions in the United States since 1973.[33] This is nearly ten times the number of Jews who perished in the Holocaust! Twenty-two percent of all pregnancies (excluding miscarriages) end in abortion.[34] The older generation has killed nearly a quarter of this new generation. This is no celebration of life but generational genocide.

- Some estimates show twenty million Americans were victims of parental incest as children. This is a particularly damaging form of sexual abuse because the individuals who perpetrate the abuse are those upon whom the victim trusts and depends.[35]

- Currently, there are over one million infected with HIV and AIDS in the United States. There have already been over five hundred thousand AIDS-related deaths—the equivalent of the entire population of Las Vegas. [36]

- Nearly 50 percent of spouses have experienced an extramarital affair.[37] Only 35 percent of the marriages survive the affair.[38] Multiply this by the number of children who have lost a parent as a result.

- Over 40 percent of all births in the United States are to unwed mothers. That is over 1.7 million illegitimate births each year.[39] That's more than the population of thirteen different states![40]

WHERE IS THE CHURCH?

These statistics can appear overwhelming but every year it actually worsens. So how can we stop this downward spiral? To begin with, the Church has been far too silent in addressing sexual sin and the collateral damage it produces. Let's be honest. The reason Christians are so quiet is that they are too often attracted to Babylon. They secretly indulge in the pleasures this kingdom offers. Many pastors and parents try to restrain themselves from yielding to the most damaging temptations for the sake of reputation and family. However, cold hearts do not attract the presence of God. As a result, most kids leave Christianity when they get older because the pleasures of Babylon were greater and more frequent than the encounters they had with God in their home and church.

Typically, the Church has either overemphasized grace and what is permissible or holiness and what is not permissible. Both yield the same result; a weakened intimacy with Christ. Intimacy is the only protection and remedy from the extremes of worldliness and religious legalism.

I remember asking a young woman if she had an interest in a particular young man. She replied, "I have an emotional interest but not a romantic interest." I believe this position describes many people's relationship with God. It wasn't always this way. At one time, their hearts were ablaze with a love for God. But there was a disappointment, an unfilled expectation, or an unexpected loss that caused them to hold back a piece of their heart from God. As a result, their relationship slowly cooled as they drifted far from their first love.

Rather than being a part of the problem, the Church must once again be a part of the solution. As we return to our first love with God, we will be able to touch those who are deeply wounded and suffering. Jesus reached out in love to the woman caught in adultery but then directed her to change her life. This culture needs more than temporary pleasure; it needs to discover something better.

Am I Not Enough?

Am I not enough, Mine own? enough,
Mine own, for thee?
Hath the world its palace towers,
Garden glades of magic flowers,
Where thou fain wouldst be?
Fair things and false are there,
False things but fair.
All shalt thou find at last,
Only in Me.
Am I not enough, Mine own? I, for ever
and alone, I, needing thee?
—Gerhard Tersteegen, 1697–1769[41]

NOTES

1. Queen, "I Want it All," *Greatest Hits II* (1989), http://www.queenwords. com/lyrics/songs/sng19_04.shtml (accessed 1/4/10).

2. "Cornel1801," http://www.cornel1801.com/video/AN02PI01.html (accessed 11/18/10).

3. Edmond Burke, *From the Wisdom of Our Fathers*, http://founderswisdom.wordpress.com/category/edmond-burke/ (accessed 1/4/10).

4. E. Stanley Jones, *The Unshakable Kingdom and the Unchanging Person* (Nashville, TN: Abingdon Press, 1972), 166.

5. "The Big Picture," *Los Angeles Times*, http://latimesblogs.latimes.com/ the_big_picture/2009/11/jim-camerons-avatar-price-tag-how-about-a-cool-500- million.html (accessed 1/4/10).

6. Ricard Lacayo, "Inside the New Dallas Cowboys Stadium," *Time*, http:// www.time.com/time/nation/article/0,8599,1924535,00.html (accessed 1/4/10).

7. "Yankees Flop in Opener at New $1.5 Billion Dollar Home," *http://nbcsports.msnbc.com/id/30252173/* (accessed 1/6/10). (accessed 11/17/10).

8. "TV Viewing at 'All Time High,' Nielsen Says," *CNN.com/ Entertainment*, http://www.cnn.com/2009/SHOWBIZ/TV/02/24/us.video.nielsen/ (accessed 1/6/10).

9. "How much money was spent on entertainment in the U.S., in 2004?," *justanswer.com*, http://www.justanswer.com/questions/jqn-money-spent-entertainment-u-s-2004 (accessed 1/6/10).

10. "Money Well Spent?," *cheathouse.com*, http://www.cheathouse.com/essay/essay_view.php?p_essay_id=102729 (accessed 1/6/10).

11. "Americans Give Record 295B to Charity," *USA Today* (2007), http://www. usatoday.com/news/nation/2007-06-25-charitable_N.htm (accessed 1/6/10).

12. "Gambling: United States," *Lycos Retriever*, http://www.lycos.com/info/ gambling--united-states.html (accessed 1/6/10).

13. GDP (gross domestic product) is the market value of all goods and services from a nation in a given year.

14. "The World Factbook, *Central Intelligence Agency*," https://www.cia.gov/ library/publications/the-world-factbook/fields/2195.html (accessed 11/18/10).

15. "Television Industry Overview," http://www.turnoffyourtv.com/networks/revenueupdate04/revenue.html (accessed 1/6/10).

16. "Russia Could Extend Defense Budget by 25 percent," *Welt Online*, (2008), http://www.welt.de/english-news/article2468669/Russia-could-extend-defense-budget-by-25-percent.html (accessed 1/6/10).

17. "2008 US video game sales reached $21.33 bln," *IT Facts*, (2009), http://www. itfacts.biz/2008-us-video-game-sales-reached-2133-bln/12439 (accessed 1/6/10).

18. "Fiscal Year 2011 Budget Estimates," *NASA*, 4, http://www.nasa.gov/pdf/420990main_FY_201_%20Budget_Overview_1_Feb_2010.pdf (accessed 11/20/10).

19. "U.S. Major Studio Film Entertainment Revenue Will Approach $42 Billion By 2011," *All Business*, (2008), http://www.allbusiness.com/media-telecommunications/movies-sound-recording/10512814-1.html (accessed 1/6/10).

20. "IFPI publishes *Recording Industry in Numbers 2010*," *IFPI*, http://www.ifpi.org/content/section_news/20100428.html (accessed 11/18/10).

21. "U.S. Radio Revenue for 2008: $16.7 Billion, down 8.5%," *Radio World*, (03/26/09), http://www.rwonline.com/article/77120 (accessed 1/6/10).

22. "Statistics and information on pornography in the USA," *Blazing Grace*, http://www.blazinggrace.org/cms/bg/pornstats (accessed 1/6/10).

23. "Fifth Committee Recommends 2008-2009 Budget of $4.17 Billion," *General Assembly*, (12/21/07) http://www.un.org/News/Press/docs/2007/gaab3835.doc.htm (accessed 1/6/10).

24. U.S. Amusement Park Attendance & Revenue History, *IAAPA*, http://www.iaapa.org/pressroom/Amusement_Park_Attendance_Revenue_History.asp (accessed 1/6/10).

25. "The World Factbook, *Central Intelligence Agency*, https://www.cia.gov/library/publications/the-world-factbook/fields/2195.html (accessed 11/18/10).

26. "The US Performing Arts Industry Includes About 9,000 Companies With Combined Annual Revenue of…," *All Business*, http://www.allbusiness.com/company-activities-management/financial/7312164-1.html (accessed 1/6/10).

27. Oriana Zill and Lowell Bergman, "Do the Math: Why the Illegal Drug Trade is Thriving," *PBS*, http://www.pbs.org/wgbh/pages/frontline/shows/drugs/special/math.html (accessed 1/6/10).

28. Steve Bonta, "Bread and Circuses," *The New American*, 10 February 2003 Used with permission.

29. George Otis Jr., "Internal Offenses, External Distractions" (Kansas City, MO: unpublished transcript of message given at National Transformation Summit, 2006).

30. Steve Bonta, "Bread and Circuses," *The New American*, 10 February 2003 Used with permission.

31. Neil Postman, *Amusing Ourselves to Death* (New York: Penguin Books, 1985), xix, xx.

32. "Sexual Abuse A Major Cause of Homosexuality?" http://www.home60515.com/3.html, (accessed 1/6/10).

33. "Abortion in the United States: Statistics and Trends," *National Right to Life*, http://www.nrlc.org/ABORTION/facts/abortionstats.html (accessed 1/6/10).

34. "Facts on Induced Abortions in the United States," *Guttmacher Institute*, http://www.guttmacher.org/pubs/fb_induced_abortion.html (accessed 4/21/10).

35. "Incest," *The National Center for Victims of Crime*, http://www.ncvc.org/ncvc/main.aspx?dbName=DocumentViewer&DocumentID=32360 (accessed 1/6/10).

36. "HIV and AIDS in America," *AVERT*, http://www.avert.org/america.htm (accessed 1/6/10).

37. "Cheating Hearts: Who's doing it and why," *Msnbc*, http://www.msnbc.msn.com/id/17951664/ (accessed 1/6/10).

38. "Infidelity Statistics," *infidelity-etc.com*, http://www.infidelity-etc.com/index.php/4 (accessed 1/6/10).

39. "Growing number of births to unwed mothers in US raises concerns," *U.S. Catholic*, http://www.uscatholic.org/news/2009/04/growing-number-births-unwed-mothers-us-raises-concerns (accessed 1/6/10).

40. "U.S. Population by State, 1790 to 2008," *infoplease*, http://www.infoplease.com/ipa/A0004986.html (accessed 1/6/10).

41. Gerhard Tersteegen, "Am I Not Enough?," *The Christian Book of Mystical Verse* (Harrisburg, PA: Christian Publications, Inc., 1963), 111.

Chapter Notes

Chapter 12

LET'S GET THIS PARTY STARTED!

I implore you in God's name, not to think of Him as hard to please,
but rather as generous beyond all that you can ask or think.
— ABBE DE TOURVILLE[1]

I came so they can have real and eternal life, more and better life
than they ever dreamed of.
—JOHN 10:10 (MSG)

My friend, Winkie Pratney, has done a biblical study on the vocations of God. One vocation is particularly interesting. He discovered that God is actually an entertainer. He demonstrated this early in the Garden of Eden. Later, He initiated various celebrations in Israel with food, music, and dance. God was interested in His people having a good time. This culminated in the joyful announcement of the Savior of the world. "Jesus appears with great joy which will come to all people and for the first time it's real, it's not fake joy; it's not manufactured. It's the real thing."[2]

Many people picture Jesus as always solemn but He is described differently in Hebrews 1:9 "Your God (Godhead), has anointed You with the oil of exultant joy *and* gladness above *and* beyond Your companions" (AMP). Let's not forget, His first miracle was at a party! Unlike Babylon, the pleasures of God do not cause a hangover the next day. They do not produce guilt and broken relationships. They don't rob of us our self worth. "The blessing of the Lord, it maketh rich, and he addeth no sorrow with it" (Prov. 10:22 KJV). There is a joy that comes from serving God that Babylon cannot replicate. This is particularly obvious when times get tough.

I have heard there are two ways to get a bone out of a dog's mouth. One is to try to pull it out and risk a nasty bite. The other is to wave a juicy steak in front of the dog's nose. Unless he's senseless, the dog will recognize the steak tastes much better. We can focus on getting Babylon out of people's mouths and risk getting our hand bit or we can testify of the goodness of our King and His Kingdom and witness people spit out their bones.

Jesus declared, "If I be lifted up, I will draw all men unto me." This was a prophetic statement of His future manner of death. However, I also believe this passage reveals that when Jesus is presented clearly for all to see, we are drawn to Him rather than away from Him. Instead of resisting the temptations of Babylon through resolution and grit, we need a fresh vision of the King and His beautiful Kingdom. Even the austere Charles Finney understood this.

> Away with this religion of resolutions! It is a snare of death. Away with this effort to make the life holy while the heart has not in it the love of God. Oh! that men would learn to look directly at Christ through the Gospel, and so close in with him by an act of loving trust as to involve a universal sympathy with his state of mind.[3]

THE BEAUTY OF HIS CREATION

If you ever get a chance to observe a sequoia pine, a male peacock, or a saltwater Mandarinfish, try to consider their source. If you go back far enough, the starting place ultimately is the mind of God. What we see in nature came originally from His creative imagination. Now consider this. According to quantum physics, everything in the universe vibrates at a certain frequency, whether it is trees, animals, or rocks. The Bible begins by telling us that "God said," and it came into existence. Everything in nature owes its existence to the resonance of His voice. God first imagined and then spoke our world into being. Amazing. When God created our world, He stepped back and said it was *very* good. No one can argue the beauty of His creation. It remains a masterpiece from the farthest galaxy to a single intricate snowflake.

King David declared, "I praise you because I am fearfully and wonderfully made..." (Ps. 139:14). God graciously gave us life but also gave us the ability to experience it abundantly in His universe. Consider for a moment how He made our physical bodies.

- God gave us the gift of sight, but then He gave us something more. He gave us the ability to distinguish color and then filled the earth with a vast array of vivid and soft colors and hues. There is color and beauty everywhere—from bright-colored flowers to a blazing sunset, from tropical butterflies to majestic mountains.

- God gave us the ability to consume necessary nutrients from nature, but then He gave us something more. He gave us the ability to sense various flavors, textures, and smells and then filled the earth with a variety of different edible substances.

- God gave us the gift of sex. He could have made it for procreation only, but He gave us something more. Unlike salmon that die after spawning, we have the ability to obtain great pleasure in what is biologically essential to our survival.

- God gave us the ability to sleep to renew our strength, but then He gave us something more. He gave us the ability to dream—to engage in creative expressions of life free from the restraints of time and space.

THE SWEETNESS OF COMMUNION

Much of the pleasure God offers is given freely to all. "He causes his sun to rise on the evil and the good, and sends rain on the righteous and the unrighteous" (Mt. 5:45). However, personal communion is reserved for those who walk in holiness (see Isa. 35:8-10). This level of relationship is the most satisfying pleasure of all. The Psalmist found great pleasure in doing what was right. "Blessed *[how happy]* is the one who does not step with the wicked or stand in the way that sinners take or sit in the company of mockers, but whose delight [pleasure] is in the law of the Lord, and who meditates on his law day and night" (Ps. 1:1–2).

God gave Eve to Adam, but He offered His friendship as well. The Scriptures tells us that God would visit Adam and Eve "in the cool of the day" (Gen. 3:8). I believe this was both morning and evening. God loved to hang out with them. This offering of Himself is the essence of the Good News. Knowing Him is eternal life (see John 17:3).

Enoch was an early descendent of Adam and Eve and the great grandfather of Noah. Not much is written of Enoch, but what we find is significant. The Bible says he "walked faithfully with God; then he was no more, because God took him away" (Gen. 5:24). Here was a man who enjoyed spending time with his God. The Lord must have found pleasure in him, because the Bible says that the Lord took him away. Now that's interesting. Can you imagine? One day Enoch was walking and talking with God and then suddenly, God promoted him to glory, not just in his spirit but in his body as well. I don't know if there was a fiery chariot like Elijah or a beautiful staircase to heaven like Jacob. Perhaps he just walked into a bright light and disappeared. I just hope someone witnessed the event so that Mrs. Enoch and the kids would know why Dad was not coming home for dinner.

Enoch was 365 years old at the time. Now that's a long time to get to know someone. I have been married for over thirty-five years, and my wife can probably finish some of my sentences. But can you imagine two persons being best friends for over 350 years? Incidentally, God did not take Enoch because he was faultless. The Bible does not say He took him because he had accomplished much on this earth. God took him to his eternal home because He so enjoyed being with him (see Heb. 11:5).

The apostle Paul desired this communion with God more than anything this life had to offer. "What is more, I consider everything a loss compared to the surpassing greatness of knowing Christ Jesus my Lord, for whose sake I have lost all things. I consider them garbage, that I may gain Christ" (Phil. 3:8).

What is remarkable is that enjoying God brings genuine pleasure to Him also. Some Christians have a hard time believing that they can be a source of God's joy and happiness. Their greatest hope would be for the Lord to say to them, "Well done, good and faithful servant!" (Matt. 25:23). Perhaps that is more than we deserve, but I believe God wants to do more. When we first see Him face to face, He may say, "Thank you, for being My friend. You have brought great joy to My heart. I am so pleased with you!" If He did, how could we not fall at His feet?

Is it possible that we can enjoy Him more than the temporal pleasures of this world? More than sports, sex, and rock and roll? If so, can we take pleasure in Him on a sustained basis? The answer is *yes we can!*

THE BLESSEDNESS OF HIS PRESENCE

There is extreme pleasure in knowing God intimately. It is so valuable that an entire book in the Bible is devoted to it. Song of Solomon vividly describes the pleasure of being with the one who has captured our hearts. "My dove in the clefts of the rock, in the hiding places on the mountainside, show me your face, let me hear your voice; for your voice is sweet, and your face is lovely" (Song 2:14). We will look at this more closely in chapter 14. Unlike other religions, the God of the Bible loves us passionately and unconditionally. All are welcomed, particularly those who have been discarded or forgotten.

King David was a man with a passion for God. He absolutely loved to be with God. "Surely you have granted him unending blessings and made him glad with the joy of your presence" (Ps. 21:6). I believe he had frequent encounters with the Holy Spirit. "You have made known to me the path of life; you will fill me with joy in your presence, with eternal pleasures at your right hand" (Ps. 16:11). King David had discovered a key to abundant life—living in His presence!

When the Holy Spirit comes, He changes everything. Our hearts begins to burn and melt. Tears begin to fall. Spiritual insight and understanding brighten the dark recesses of our minds. We find our spirits flowing tenderly, thoughtfully, and lovingly. We become filled with a joy unspeakable.

A newfound love for others is set ablaze in our hearts. We do not just feel for them; we deeply feel God's love for them. This love compels us to tell them the Good News. We want them to encounter God for themselves. The Great Commission can only be accomplished through the love and power of the Holy Spirit. He is the perfect one: perfect in love, perfect in wisdom, and perfect in power.

By design, we are to love and be loved. This comes from the very nature of God Himself. The Godhead enjoys intimate communion among the Father, Son, and Holy Spirit and wants us to enjoy this also. Jesus prayed, "My prayer is not for them alone. I pray also for those who will believe in me through their message, that all of them may be one, Father, just as you are in me and I am in you. May they also be in us so that the world may believe that you have sent me" (John 17:20-21).

Years ago, I had an encounter with God that ushered me into His throne room. While there, His love overwhelmed me. At one point, I tried to grasp the negative emotions I often experienced on earth. I remembered the words but discovered that it was impossible to experience the sensations associated them. I discovered that the parental affection of our heavenly Father dispels all fear, doubt, and anxiety. He is the true rest and joy of our desire.

> Fairest Lord Jesus, Ruler of all nature,
> O Thou of God and man the Son,
> Thee will I cherish, Thee will I honor,
> Thou, my soul's glory, joy and crown.

> Fair are the meadows, fairer still the woodlands,
> Robed in the blooming garb of spring;
> Jesus is fairer, Jesus is purer,
> Who makes the woeful heart to sing.

> Fair is the sunshine,
> Fairer still the moonlight,
> And all the twinkling starry host;

> Jesus shines brighter, Jesus shines purer
> Than all the angels heaven can boast.[4]

Notes

1. Abbe de Tourville, *Quotes About God*, http://www.tentmaker.org/Quotes/ godquotes.htm (accessed 1/16/11).

2. Winkie Pratney, *Finding 35 Major Vocations Given by God Rooted in His Nature*, http://www.crossrhythms.co.uk/articles/life/Winkie_Pratney_ Finding_35_major_vocations_given_by_God_rooted_in_his_nature/37162/p1/ (accessed 1/14/11).

3. Charles Finney, *How to Overcome Sin*, http://www.gospeltruth. net/1868_75Independent/740101_overcome_sin.htm (accessed 1/16/11).

4. German Jesuits, "Fairest Lord Jesus," (1677), http://www.cyberhymnal. org/htm/f/a/l/faljesus.htm (accessed 3/5/10).

Chapter Notes

Part Three

THE ROAD TO VICTORY

Chapter 13

Increasing Spiritual Authority

You are but a poor soldier of Christ if you think you can overcome without fighting and suppose you can have the crown without conflict.
—John Chrysostom[1]

God is strong, and he wants you strong. So take everything the Master has set out for you, well-made weapons of the best materials...
—Ephesians 6:10–11 (MSG)

All Christians have had confrontations with Babylon's power but often with limited success. One of the problems is that they frequently deal with the threat passively. Have you ever been followed by a threatening dog in an unfamiliar neighborhood? Typically, we try to ignore the dog, hoping it will lose interest and leave us alone. If that does not work, we may try to use a nonthreatening voice with an extended hand, hoping he will stop snarling and barking. If that fails, we may finally resort to turning around abruptly, stomping our foot, and sternly commanding the dog, "Go home!" We might even pick up a rock or stick to frighten the dog.

This third method reflects the attitude we must have with the kingdom of Babylon. Many are trying the first two passive methods, but it is hopeless. Babylon will not respond to anything but authority, true spiritual authority. The apostle Paul understood this.

> The world is unprincipled. It's dog-eat-dog out there! The world doesn't fight fair. But we don't live or fight our battles that way—never have and never will. The tools of our trade aren't for marketing or manipulation, but *they are for demolishing that entire massively corrupt culture*. We use our powerful God-tools for smashing warped philosophies, tearing down barriers erected against the truth of God, fitting every loose thought and emotion and impulse into the structure of life shaped by Christ. Our tools are ready at hand for clearing the ground of every obstruction and building lives of obedience into maturity (2 Cor. 10:3–6 MSG).

How do we obtain the power to overcome the "massively corrupt culture"? Genuine spiritual power comes from true spiritual authority. This God-given spiritual authority can be obtained in three basic ways.

I. The Gift of Inheritance

First, we receive spiritual authority through inheritance. We possess spiritual authority as individuals created in the image of God. This is rediscovered when we are born again. In the early Church, we see an example of this in the physical realm. The apostle Paul's life and message caused a religious riot in Jerusalem. The Roman soldiers intervened but determined to flog him for additional information. Prior to applying this cruel form of interrogation, Paul said something that changed everything.

> As they stretched him out to flog him, Paul said to the centurion standing there, "Is it legal for you to flog a Roman citizen who hasn't even been found guilty?" When the centurion heard this, he went to the commander and reported it. "What are you going to do?" he asked. "This man is a Roman citizen." The commander went to Paul and asked, "Tell me, are you a Roman citizen?" "Yes, I am," he answered. Then the commander said, "I had to pay a big price for my citizenship." "But I was born a citizen," Paul replied. Those who were about to question him withdrew

immediately. The commander himself was alarmed when he realized that he had put Paul, a Roman citizen, in chains (Acts 22:25–29).

Paul's position as a Roman citizen made a huge impact on the powers aligned against him. They had to submit to the rights Paul possessed.

Paul's authority was recognized and respected not only by the Roman Empire but also in the kingdom of darkness. In another situation, some religious leaders envied Paul's spiritual authority. They tried to see the same miracles invoking the name of Jesus as Paul did.

> A team of itinerant Jews who were traveling from town to town casting out demons planned to experiment by using the name of the Lord Jesus. The incantation they decided on was this: "I adjure you by Jesus, whom Paul preaches, to come out!" Seven sons of Sceva, a Jewish priest, were doing this. But when they tried it on a man possessed by a demon, the demon replied, "I know Jesus and I know Paul, but who are you?" And he leaped on two of them and beat them up, so that they fled out of his house naked and badly injured (Acts 19:13–16 TLB).

Paul was known in hell but his spiritual position was not unique. All those who are born again are *citizens* of the Kingdom of God (see Eph. 2:19). As citizens, you possess this type of spiritual authority. If you remain faithful to God, you will always possess it. "To the one who is victorious and does my will to the end, I will give authority over the nations" (Rev. 2:26). However, you are more than an ordinary Kingdom citizen; you are also *ambassadors* of the Kingdom (see 2 Cor. 5:20). Like the early Church, you have the authority to represent Christ and His Kingdom in the face of all other powers. In addition, we are *sons and daughters* of our heavenly Father (see 2 Cor. 6:18). This makes our position incredibly powerful. As a result, we should never underestimate or undervalue it. "These, then, are the things you should teach. Encourage and rebuke with all authority. Do not let anyone despise you" (Titus 2:15).

Satan often attempts to convince us that we have no authority because of our past sins, weaknesses, and failures. He is desperately trying to keep us from exercising our spiritual authority against him. He greatly fears our command to, "Go home!"

II. THE BLESSING OF IMPARTATION

Second, we receive spiritual authority through impartation. This authority is given as an additional blessing to those seeking empowerment for service. This happens in a certain place at a certain time. "When Jesus had called the Twelve together, he gave them power and authority to drive out all demons and to cure diseases, and he sent them out to preach the kingdom of God and to heal the sick… So they set out and went from village to village, proclaiming the good news and healing people everywhere" (Luke 9:1–2, 6). The disciples received a special impartation of power from Jesus for their assigned mission task. Pentecost was another example of this. Jesus instructed them to wait in Jerusalem for the Holy Spirit to come upon them (see Acts 1:4–5). This was an essential element in fulfilling their spiritual calling. It would give them keen spiritual insight and additional authority to proclaim the message of the Kingdom throughout the world. After Pentecost, they went out and prayed for others to receive this impartation.

Another example of this is when the church elders commissioned Paul's young disciple, Timothy. Later, the apostle Paul reminded Timothy of the importance of that event. "Do not neglect the gift which is in you, [that special inward endowment] which was directly *imparted* to you [by the Holy Spirit] by prophetic utterance when the elders laid their hands upon you [at your ordination]" (1 Tim. 4:14 AMP). Throughout the epistles, the early Church was encouraged to seek for the impartation of the gifts of the Spirit. This enabled them to be more effective in penetrating the kingdom of Babylon and replacing it with the Kingdom of God.

There was also an impartation of spiritual authority on a few humble believers in 1906. From a simple urban mission on Azusa Street in Los Angeles, the Pentecostal Movement has spread throughout the world. Sadly, many of the denominations that came out of this movement have become negligent in pursuing this spiritual impartation. They are embracing the values of Babylon rather than gaining more spiritual authority. In this desperate hour, we need more, not less, of this spiritual impartation.

I have been to Christian conferences and meetings where there was a strong awareness of God's presence. This has produced a greater spiritual impartation among those present. After the meeting, many have returned home with this awareness. They have discovered increased spiritual authority in their home and at their job. It is an indispensable weapon against the kingdom of Babylon.

III. THE REWARD FOR OBEDIENCE

Last, we may receive spiritual authority as a reward for our obedience. This authority is available to all believers but is contingent upon a person's conduct and lifestyle. In these next few chapters, I want to explain the significance of obeying our calling to intimacy, disengagement, and rulership.

There are some believers who want to focus on the spiritual authority obtained only though inheritance and impartation and neglect this third way. In doing so, they may even experience some positive results for a time, but it takes more than power to penetrate Babylon and replace it with God's Kingdom—it takes favor with God.

"Not everyone who says to me, 'Lord, Lord,' will enter the kingdom of heaven, but only he who *does the will* of my Father who is in heaven. Many will say to me on that day, 'Lord, Lord, did we not prophesy in your name, and in your name drive out demons and perform many miracles?' Then I will tell them plainly, 'I never knew you'" (Matt. 7:21–23). Miracles and power were never meant to be a true indicator of God's favor or pleasure. If we want to honor Him and fulfill His desires, we must do His work His way.

PRAYER

Lord God, help equip me with all the giftings and weapons You have made available. Give me the skill to use them effectively for Your service. Deliver me from passivity and man-pleasing! I want my spirit to be as bold as a lion and my heart as gentle as a lamb. Make me an irrepressible force for good in this world. May my faithful obedience bring fame to Your name and joy to Your heart. Amen.

NOTES

1. John Chrysostom, *Daily Christian Quote*, http://dailychristianquote.com/dcqspiritwarfare2.html (accessed 3/310).

Chapter Notes

Chapter 14

FINDING THE KING'S HEART

The kingdom of God is a kingdom of love; and love is never a stagnant pool.
—HENRY W. DuBOSE[1]

My heart says of you, "Seek his face!" Your face, Lord, I will seek.
—PSALM 27:8

Queen Esther discovered that the Jews were facing systematic and widespread extermination. They were about to be slaughtered through the misdirected decree of her husband, King Xerxes. Esther chose to risk her life by appealing for mercy from the king. Fortunately, King Xerxes responded favorably and an entire nation survived. What gave her such influence in the kingdom? It was her intimate relationship with the king. Spiritual authority increases with our intimacy with the King.

Sadly, many Christians are more like Lot's wife than Queen Esther. By God's grace, Lot's wife received a way of escape from impending judgment.

She took the right path, but her heart was not in it. She was still attached to another kingdom. Tragically, Lot's wife could not refuse her divided heart any longer. She looked back and was instantly turned to a pillar of salt. Lot's wife became a monument to the foolishness of following God in deed but not in heart.

Today, many people are looking to God for deliverance but without intimacy. They want blessings but not intimacy. They want heaven but not intimacy. I remember meeting a man in the urban core who expressed a desire to follow Christ but was constantly a no-show when it came to going to church or fellowship with other Christian brothers. I expressed my disappointment to God and heard Him say, "He only wants a piece of Me." What a tragic statement! Can you imagine people want only a piece of God? Can you imagine the disappointment God feels when we are only interested in what He can do for us and ignore intimacy with Him? "You refuse to listen when I call and no one pays attention when I stretch out my hand" (Prov. 1:24).

EVERYTHING FLOWS FROM INTIMACY

You cannot represent the Kingdom of God unless you know the King. If we desire to know the King, it is imperative that we know His desires. What is His treasured desire? In Song of Solomon 6, God says, "Our eyes overwhelm Him." In chapter 7, He reveals, "How beautiful and pleasing" we are to Him. In chapter 8, we discover, "He loves even the sound of our voice." The King desires an intimate relationship with us. We are the joy of His desire!

He is desperate for our affections. When we respond to Him, something wonderful happens—we give Him the freedom to be Himself. No longer does our coldness limit Him. He is able to share His feelings and secrets because we no longer are His servants but His friends. When we respond to Him, something else happens—we become free also. Our spirits rise and take flight when His desires and our desires become one.

Intimacy is the key to victory over the world, the flesh, and the devil. Like the sun that causes all other stars to disappear in its glory, so our relationship with Christ is able to outshine all the allurements of Babylon. The gravitational pull of His heart will keep us from spinning out of orbit into the darkness of discouragement, the coldness of deception, and the color-less life of religious legalism. The tenderness of His love provides light to our path and warmth for our journey.

Like good and faithful Boaz who redeemed the poor widow Ruth, so we have been rescued from spiritual poverty into an abundant way of living. Intimacy with the King washes away the guilt of our past, releases us from stresses of today's world, and raises us above all fears of the future. The most encouraging realization in humanity's struggles is found in an old, familiar Sunday school song, "Jesus loves me, this I know."

A LIGHT UPON A HILL

Moses had a life-changing experience with God at the burning bush on Mount Horeb. God then instructed him to bring the Children of Israel to the same location from Egypt (see Ex. 3:12). After the ten plagues, Moses was finally able to lead God's people to this place of destiny. As they drew closer, Moses must have anticipated they would soon experience the same life-changing encounter with God.

Unfortunately, when God revealed Himself, the people became fearful and pleaded that Moses act as a mediator on their behalf (see Ex. 20:18–19). They were content to get religious instructions without any intimacy with God. They wanted a peripheral connection rather than a personal relationship.

Moses did as they requested and Jehovah blessed him. Through subsequent encounters with the Lord, his face became radiant because of his proximity to God's glory. Talk about an enlightening experience! Imagine Mrs. Moses telling the kids to cut the lights because it is their bedtime, only to have them respond, "The lights are already out, Mom—it's Dad again!" However, there was another problem. I have always assumed that Moses wore a veil to shield others from the glory emitting from his face. Recently my daughter showed me another interesting reason. In Exodus 34:33–35, we get the context.

> When Moses finished speaking to them, he put a veil over his face. But whenever he entered the Lord's presence to speak with him, he removed the

veil until he came out. And when he came out and told the Israelites what he had been commanded, they saw that his face was radiant. Then Moses would put the veil back over his face until he went in to speak with the Lord.

Notice that Moses would speak to the Israelites with his face uncovered. In other words, Moses was not trying to hide the glory from the people. So why would he use a veil? The answer is found in 2 Corinthians 3:13, "Unlike Moses, we have nothing to hide. Everything is out in the open with us. He wore a veil so the children of Israel *wouldn't notice that the glory was fading away ...*" (MSG).

Moses did not place a veil over his face because of what he had but because of what he did not have. He was trying to hide the fact that the glory was fading. Why was it fading? Because too much time had passed since he had been in the Lord's presence. Moses' diminishing glory was not because of God's delay in blessing but because of Moses' delay in seeking. Moses' lack of initiative was behind the fading glory. Today, many Christians are wearing veils and masks to hide their fading glory. We need to revisit our prayer altars and restore His glory in our lives.

THE GAZE SUSTAINS

To deepen our intimacy, we must learn to seek His face intently. In Revelation 4, we find a beautiful emerald rainbow surrounding a throne constantly emitting rumblings, lightning, and thunder. Try to imagine the power and the splendor of this scene! Four living creatures also encircle the throne. These are not angels but some other type of spiritual being. These awesome creatures declare night and day, "Holy, holy, holy is the Lord God Almighty, who was, and is, and is to come" (Rev. 4:8). Let me ask you, how are they able to worship on such a sustained basis? The key is they are gazing upon the Unchanging One who sits upon the throne. Their gaze sustains them.

Peter was able to ignore the storm and walk upon the water when his focus was on Jesus. Only when he took his eyes off Jesus did he begin to sink. Can you imagine the futility of Peter's friends jumping in the sea and trying to sustain Peter on top of the water? People cannot sustain us—only Christ can. Peter's gaze sustained him.

Most of us face challenges daily at home, work, and school. When our focus is on other people or circumstances around us, we eventually start to sink. The only way we can avoid sinking is to focus on the one who stands above the storm. He is also the only one who will sustain us. "Let us run with endurance the race that is set before us, *fixing* our eyes on Jesus" (Heb 12:1–2 NASB). Our gaze will sustain us!

Tuning Our Ears

To increase our intimacy, we also need to tune our ears to God's voice. We will increase our attentiveness as we decrease the distractions of other conflicting voices. Many pride themselves in being able to multitask, but it is killing our spiritual lives. We must reduce the distractions and tune in to Him. "The message of the Kingdom has never changed; we just stopped listening before God was done talking."[2]

We must be led by His voice rather than what we perceive with our natural eyes. I believe there is a darkness coming to this earth, and if we walk by sight, we will be lost. In the kingdom of Babylon, "seeing is believing," but in the Kingdom of God, "faith comes from hearing" (Rom. 10:27 KJV). Many who met Jesus insisted on seeing before they would believe, including the Jews, the religious leaders, and King Herod. They were looking when they should have been listening.

Jesus continually admonished, "He who has ears to hear, let him hear." I believe He was exhorting the people to pay close attention to what He was saying; to listen carefully to what He was communicating. Jesus knew there was a distinction between hearing words and listening. It takes greater attentiveness and effort to listen. My wife lets me know if I am hearing her but not listening! We need to evaluate honestly our level of attentiveness to His voice. Are we hearing or actually listening to Jesus? Are we living with our ears tuned to His voice? Do we quickly respond when He calls? "My sheep *listen* to my voice; I know them, and they follow me" (John 10:27).

Physicists are increasingly converting scientific data into sounds. They are doing this because the ear is incredibly sensitive to the slightest changes in pitch. Hearing is more sensitive and accurate than sight. Mary only recognized Jesus at the empty tomb when He spoke her name. Peter was only willing to jump out of the boat into the stormy seas when he heard Jesus say, "Come." Even when we arrive in heaven, we will immediately recognize His voice rather than His physical appearance.

In science, the closer we are to an energy source, the louder it becomes. However, scientists have also discovered the closer we are to a source of energy, the lower is its resonance. In Romans, Paul speaks of the Holy Spirit who aids us in prayer "with groanings too deep for words" (Rom. 6:26 NASB). Many have heard His cry, but are we close enough to hear His groan? He wants to draw us into an intimacy that is beyond words.

IN HIS STEPS

To strengthen our intimacy, we must be willing to walk in His footsteps. When Jesus began His ministry, He instructed His future disciples, "Come, follow me." He wanted them to go where He was going. When blind Bartimaeus cried for help, Jesus directed His disciples to bring him to where Jesus was. Bartimaeus could not get face-to-face with Jesus by sitting where he was at; he needed to move. Jesus' message to those who were hurting was *"Come to me,* all you who are weary and burdened, and I will give you rest"* (Matt. 11:28).

Why should we go to Jesus rather than attempting to get Him to come to us? Because He said, "I know where I came from and where I am going. But you have no idea where I come from or where I am going" (John 8:14). More than anyone else, Jesus knows where He is going. Consequently, we must change direction, not Him. Most people hate to admit they are going the wrong way, especially men when they are driving. To ask for help and change direction can be humbling, but it is the only way to get on the right road.

This is in sharp contrast to the pleas from the pulpit, "Just ask Jesus to *come* into your heart." I know Jesus will always respond to a hungry and sincere heart, but we should be directing people to *follow* Him. Some are willing to follow Him but only under the right conditions. When the road becomes steep and rough, most think it is time to take another path. They are willing to follow Him beside the still waters but not up Calvary's road.

THE WEDDING REQUISITE

The parable of the ten virgins in Matthew 25 tells us that all the virgins were anxiously awaiting the bridegroom at the marriage feast. However, five of the virgins were foolish because they had failed to bring sufficient oil for their lamps. They must have assumed others could simply supply their shortfall. Regrettably, their assumption was wrong, and they had to go back to town to purchase more. While gone, the bridegroom was drawn to the lamps of the wise virgins that penetrated the dark night. When He arrived, they went in and the door was shut. On returning, the foolish virgins tried to gain entry, but the bridegroom made a tragic pronouncement, *"I don't know you."*

This statement is the ultimate price of insufficient intimacy. Our commitment to seeking His face, listening for His voice, and following in His steps will ultimately determine whether Christ will know us. You cannot inherit it or acquire it from others. You can only obtain this oil of intimacy through personal experience.

NO PRIESTS ALLOWED

The reason many Christians are struggling today is because they have neglected intimacy and have become overly dependent on others for their spiritual health. As the five foolish virgins discovered, there is coming a day when you can no longer depend on someone else to carry you. When Timothy was struggling with fear, Paul did not tell him to find some anointed preacher and have them lay hands on him. Rather, he told Timothy to "fan into flame the gift" that God had already given him. In other words, Timothy needed to take initiative to get his help directly from the Lord. Spiritual maturity is developed when people find God for themselves, not when they stand in line for a quick fix.

In Old Testament times, the priest served as a mediator between God and His people. The people could not go into the holy places of the temple but were dependent on the priests to represent them before the Lord. When Christ died, the curtain in the holy place ripped in two. This signified a change in the manner in which people would have access to God. Followers of the Lord would no longer be dependent on a mediator; they now had direct access.

The newly appointed pastors of the early Church served as shepherds to the people who were often referred to as sheep. People understood the analogy because it was a popular occupation in Israel. In raising sheep, shepherds will protect the flock, lead them to green pastures, and bring them safely back to the sheep pen. However, shepherds do not directly feed the sheep. When Jesus told Peter to feed His sheep three times (see John 21:17), the word "feed," meant to "pasture."[3] A shepherd does not pull grass, pre-chew it, and stuff it in the sheep's mouths. *Sheep must learn to eat for themselves to become strong and healthy.*

In most churches, believers want the spiritual leader to pay the price of intimacy with God. They then expect anointed preaching and prayers from their pastor to solve their problems. Members of the congregation are often more interested in the impartation of a blessing than finding closeness and intimacy with God themselves. They often try to obtain an anointing; ignoring that deep trust and intimacy transcends anointing. The gifts of God are not a substitute for intimacy with Him. "If I have the gift of prophecy and can fathom all mysteries and all knowledge, and if I have a faith that can move mountains, but do not have love, I am nothing" (1 Cor. 13:2). Without the intimacy, we have nothing.

This is why revivals have been so difficult to sustain. Revivals should create greater opportunities to experience God and produce a call to a deeper and more intimate walk with Him. Unfortunately, they often become too dependent on a particular Christian personality and facility. In many events, the focus is on a charismatic person rather than God. The leaders often enjoy the attention, and the attendees often prefer to circumvent their spiritual responsibilities. This co-dependency produces the seeds of the revival's demise.

When the constant focus is on spiritual personalities in the Body of Christ, division and competition are inevitable. The apostle Paul had to address this issue with the Corinthian Church. "My brothers, some from Chloe's household have informed me that there are quarrels among you. What I mean is this: One of you says, 'I follow Paul'; another, 'I follow Apollos'; another, 'I follow Cephas'; still another, 'I follow Christ'" (1 Cor. 1:11–12). There must be a better way of thinking in the Body of Christ.

TEST OF INTIMACY

One day Peter made a bold prediction, "Even if all fall away ... I will not." He followed by saying "Even if I have to die with you, I will never disown you." But Jesus saw a flaw in Peter's claims and warned him of his future denial (see Matt. 26:33–25). What did Jesus know that Peter did not? Peter's love was conditional.

Peter's love was dependent on receiving. This is why Peter stayed beside Jesus until the day He was arrested. To others he looked like a faithful servant, a close confidant, and spiritually perceptive. Nevertheless, all along Peter was receiving from the Lord. When the soldiers arrested Jesus and took Him to the high priest, Peter stayed at a safe distance. Why? Because he was interested enough to observe but not intimate enough to help.

Here is the critical issue. In that midnight hour, Peter was no longer in a position of receiving; now he needed to give. The problem was Peter had nothing to give. He was now completely alone, without anyone to tell him what he should do or say. All he could draw from was his own well. The problem was that his well was dry. He could not give what he did not have.

Before this event, Peter was very confident in himself. He even promised to follow Jesus unto death. What he failed to promise, because he did not yet see the value, was *his love*. Jesus saw Peter's heart, and it took going through a midnight hour for Peter to see the shallowness of his love. This revelation broke Peter's heart. [4]

Nevertheless, after Christ's death, Peter's focus was on receiving once again. Peter and his friends decided to go fishing. In the morning, Jesus appeared on the shore and told the disciples to throw their nets on the other side of the boat. Through this specific instruction, Jesus demonstrated to Peter who his source would always be. In a brief period, their nets became full of fish. Peter and his friends then responded to Jesus' invitation for a shore lunch and fellowship.

After the meal, Jesus revealed a deeper purpose for His visit. Jesus did not ask Peter to reconfirm his faithful service or willingness to lay down his life. Jesus was interested in that one important and unresolved issue. He needed to know the depth of Peter's love—if he loved Him supremely.

Peter's response was that he loved Him as a dear friend. Jesus repeated the question and Peter repeated his response. Finally, Jesus asked Peter if he only considered Him a dear friend, to which Peter embarrassingly admitted it was the extent of his love. Why was Christ so interested in the depth of Peter's love? Because "Christ is unwilling to entrust his little ones to one who does not love him."[5]

Jesus did not ask Peter because He did not know the answer but because He was showing Peter what he lacked. This conversation probably took place in the presence of the other disciples. Jesus was sending them all a clear message on the importance of intimacy. This encounter also revealed the incredible importance of Pentecost. When they began to meet in the upper room, they no doubt recalled their final contacts with Jesus. This shore lunch encounter probably spurred some deep soul-searching on the part of those present. They knew they needed to love Jesus at a greater level but perhaps struggled in knowing how. Likely, their prayers for intimacy grew with their desperation. It was in answer to these prayers that their hearts were satisfied in the coming of the Holy Spirit.

We have already mentioned that the Holy Spirit came first as a wind to penetrate Babylonian values and replace them with the values of God's Kingdom, but in the second phase, there was fire. What did the fire represent? Song of Solomon 8:6–7 describes our love for God: "It burns like blazing fire, like a mighty flame. Many waters cannot quench love; rivers cannot wash it away." This mighty fire was not a single collective flame but smaller flames resting separately upon each person. This fiery love is powerful *and* personal. After Pentecost, the disciples' love for Christ was unquenchable.

THE CATALYST OF INTIMATE PRAYER

Earlier we mentioned the four living creatures around the throne of God. Day and night, they declare God's majesty. However, there is a wider circle of twenty-four elders—each with their own throne. These elders have golden crowns that they lay before the great throne. When the Lamb of God appears and takes the scroll from His Father, the four creatures and twenty-four elders fall before Him with harps and golden bowls full of incense. The Bible says that the incense is the *prayers of the saints*. Both the creatures and the elders burst out into song with the presentation of the incense. A chain reaction has now begun in heaven! Soon millions of angels appear around the throne and join in the rapturous music. Before long, all the creatures in heaven and earth become part of this awesome chorus.

My question is, how critical were the prayers of the saints in this dramatic scene in heaven? Could our prayers actually be a catalyst for this kind of joyful response? Can our intimate and persistent communication with Jesus create a chain reaction of blissful celebration around the throne? If so, let us call upon Him with hearts ablaze for the sake of the King and His eternal Kingdom!

O Jesus, King Most Wonderful

O Jesus, King most wonderful,
Thou Conqueror renowned,
Thou Sweetness most ineffable,
In whom all joys are found!

When once Thou visitest the heart,
Then truth begins to shine,
Then earthly vanities depart,
Then kindles love divine.

O Jesus, Light of all below!
Thou Fount of life and fire!
Surpassing all the joys we know,
And all we can desire,—

May every heart confess Thy Name,
And ever Thee adore,
And, seeking Thee, itself inflame
To seek Thee more and more.

Thee may our tongues for ever bless,
Thee may we love alone,
And ever in our lives express
The image of Thine own.

—Bernard of Clairvaux, 1091–1153[6]

NOTES

1.   Henry W. DuBose , *The Quotable Christian*, http://www.pietyhilldesign. com/gcq/quotepages/godskingdom.html (accessed 2/26/10).

2.   Molly VanHeel, 4/20/10

3.   NT:1006 bo/skw **bosko** (bos'-ko); a prol. form of a primary verb [compare NT:977, NT:1016]; to pasture; *Biblesoft's New Exhaustive Strong's Numbers and Concordance with Expanded Greek-Hebrew Dictionary*. Copyright © 1994, 2003, 2006 Biblesoft, Inc. and International Bible Translators, Inc.

4.   Molly VanHeel, "Bethany Urban Development News," 10/09.

5.   From *The Wycliffe Bible Commentary*, Electronic Database. Copyright © 1962 by Moody Press. All rights reserved.

6.   Bernard of Clairvaux, "O Jesus, King Most Wonderful," *The Christian Book of Mystical Verse* (Harrisburg, PA: Christian Publications, Inc., 1963), 95–96.

Chapter Notes

_____

_____

_____

_____

_____

_____

_____

_____

_____

_____

_____

_____

_____

_____

_____

_____

Chapter 15

Renouncing Babylon

*Did I hear the words of the higher man say Babylon your throne gone down,
gone down Babylon your throne gone down.*
—Bob Marley[1]

Leave Babylon, flee from the Babylonians! …
—Isaiah 48:20

One day, I remember reaching to the back of a cluttered closet. Suddenly something pierced my finger. I recoiled and discovered a large splinter from a rough board had penetrated the tip of my finger beneath my fingernail. The splinter had gone all the way down to the base of my nail! A piece of it stuck out the top, but I could see the remainder through my fingernail.

All I could think about was getting the thing out. I pulled firmly on the exposed piece, but shockingly, only the top half came out. Now I was in trouble. How in the world was I going to get the rest out? Tweezers were worthless. I could not squeeze it out, and I could not leave it in to become infected. The thought of going to the doctor made me shudder thinking of how he would deal with my finger!

My finger throbbed as I became more desperate. Finally, I hatched a plan. Why not file my fingernail in half and then just lift it out? All I needed was a file and some time. Initially it went well as I filed quickly through my fingernail. There was virtually no pain as I made a groove the length of it. Filing deeper, the pain surfaced and soon became excruciating. That was when the blood began to flow, to the point where I could barely see my progress. It seemed to take forever to make the groove wide and deep enough to remove the rest of the splinter. Finally, it came out. I was completely relieved as I washed my wounded finger and applied disinfectant. My finger hurt, and it took several weeks before it looked normal again.

When I remember this painful experience, I think of the necessity of removing the values of Babylon out of our lives. We cannot ignore the danger we are in; we cannot hope it will leave on its own. We must remove our "wicked ways," like a foreign object in our body. If not, it will cause infection and eventually death. Spiritual authority increases as we disengage from the world's system.

Today, the Church often makes great efforts to comfort those who are hurting. Many people are struggling and pastors are trying to encourage them. That is certainly admirable, but sometimes people are hurting because they are living contrary to the Kingdom of God. If we want these people delivered from their pain, then they must also disengage from any "ways" that are hurting them.

THE QUALIFICATION FOR KINGDOM CITIZENSHIP

Many foreigners visit the United States each year. During their stay, they may pick up some of the language and culture, but they still have only limited rights in United States. The reason is understandable. It is not enough to visit national landmarks or stay with friends in the United States. It is not even enough to become familiar with U. S. history and the country's political process. These visitors simply cannot possess the rights of a United States citizen unless they follow a precise naturalization process. This process culminates with a solemn oath of allegiance. In this oath, there is a renouncing of all allegiances to any foreign state.

The Kingdom of God operates in a similar fashion. Many believers have become familiar with the Christian culture. They have learned its language, music, and priorities. They may have followed the rules respectfully and supported a church with their tithe. Nevertheless, despite all these efforts, they are still not citizens of the Kingdom of God. Why? Because their lives demonstrate they have not renounced the kingdom of Babylon and turned from its ways.

THE FALLACY OF DUAL CITIZENSHIP

Citizens of the United States often visit other countries. To do so, they must always carry a passport to prove they are citizens of their home country. There is an exception, however—a dual-citizenship status for those who qualify. This provides the unique advantage of being able to move freely between two countries and enjoy the privileges of citizenship in both.

One night, I was relaxing in front of a coffee shop we ran in the urban core. Suddenly, a stranger walked up to me and offered me some cocaine. Instinctively, I began to tell to him that I was a minister and the proprietor of the coffee shop. Barely blinking an eye, the man changed his demeanor. He started talking more energetically and began to use Christian terminology. Quickly, he pulled out a New Testament from his back pocket and started waving it with passion! He was now trying to convince me of his loyalty to God's Kingdom. It would have been funny if it were not so tragic. What was his problem? He was attempting to demonstrate a dual-citizenship status, but it was too obvious. It was a sham, a ruse, and simply unconvincing. He had failed to learn an important fact: there is no dual citizenship status in the Kingdom of God.

This reality will challenge the lifestyles of many who claim to be followers of Christ. We need to examine ourselves at home, at work, or when we are alone rather than just at church. The results will soon reveal what we spend our money on, what we most like to talk about, and what we put on our Facebook profile. Sadly, it appears many who claim to be followers of Christ are trying to be citizens of two kingdoms. They want acceptance by the world as well as the Church. They are not aliens to this culture, like the disciples after Pentecost. The Church may know them, but the world recognizes them as one of their own.

This is a common problem throughout history. "'Now then,' said Joshua, 'throw away the foreign gods that are among you and yield your hearts to the Lord, the God of Israel.' And the people said to Joshua, 'We will serve the Lord our God and obey him'" (Josh 24:23–24). The Israelites may have attempted to portray a holy zeal, but I find their response a bit disingenuous. They avoided a specific commitment to put away their foreign gods. They just added God to their religious belief system. They preferred to add one kingdom to another rather than replace one kingdom with another, but dual citizenship was never an option in God's plan! History has shown that the Israelites failed to disengage from their foreign gods, which ultimately led to their downfall.

IN THE WORLD BUT NOT OF THE WORLD

After twenty-four years in Canaan, Abraham was reminded by God that he was still an alien in the land (see Gen. 17:8). The Bible states that Abraham continued to be an alien thirty-eight years later (see Gen. 23:4). Even when he was very old, Abraham understood the importance of having his son Isaac marry someone from among his own extended family (see Gen. 24:3–4). Until the day he died, Abraham never did fit in with the local culture and lifestyle. Abraham was a man committed to being separate and never avoided the reality that he was a foreigner—an outsider. This determination was one of his greatest strengths.

Later, in the book of 1 Peter, we have the elder apostle admonishing the early Church to regard themselves as strangers and foreigners on earth. He does not do this once or twice but actually three times (see 1 Pet. 1:1, 17; 2:11)! This is significant. Peter saw the necessity of not allowing this world to dictate our values. He knew, by experience, that God's Kingdom should so captivate our minds and hearts that any other kingdom will appear strange and foreign to us. Consequently, the other kingdoms should regard us as strangers to them.

Jesus told His disciples to wait in Jerusalem until the Holy Spirit came. I do not believe the location was random or insignificant. They were directed to seek God in the midst of a vibrant and diverse city, amongst a strong religious culture controlled by an oppressive military government. This is where they would have a historic encounter with the Holy Spirit. When the Spirit fell on the 120 believers gathered in the upper room, they unknowingly formed the perfect metaphor for the Christian life. They were in the world but not of the world. Their encounter caused a separation from the culture and a corresponding penetration of that culture. As a result, a world-changing movement began that has never been equaled or surpassed.

SET APART

The great prophet Elijah wore a garment of hair and a leather belt around his waist (see 2 Kings 1). He lived a "set apart" lifestyle and was not a slave to the values of the kingdom of Babylon. In his final miracle, before his dramatic departure from this earth, he faced the dominating power of this world's system. Twice King Ahaziah's soldiers came to take Elijah. On both occasions, they died by fire from heaven. On the third attempt, the captain fell on his knees before Elijah begging for mercy. Only when the powers of this world's system had humbled themselves did Elijah agree to go with them. This was a final reminder that God's Kingdom bows to no one.

John Mulinde is a national church leader in Uganda. In his book, *Transforming Your World*, he illustrates the need to be set apart for God through the account of Daniel, Shadrach, Meshach, and Abednego in Babylon.

> They began to pray. It did not happen overnight, but in the privacy of their rooms, God began to come to them. He began to anoint them, release gifts into their lives, give them dreams and visions, wisdom, and the gift of interpretation. These things happened privately, as if they had nothing to do with the empire, but that is the way God began to work. When He finds a person who will set himself apart from the system, He begins to work in his life and in due course, God does two things:
>
> 1. *God promotes him to a place where he can begin to speak and be heard in his community.* Daniel and his friends were placed among the wise men but they were the least among them … They looked insignificant, but that is often how it starts.
> 2. *God brings crisis.* Crisis is His method of promotion.[2]

The king of Babylon had a dream, and no one could interpret it. As a result, Daniel and his friends faced death until Daniel spoke up and said that God would give the interpretation.

> Did Daniel and his friends begin to fast and pray only when the crisis came? Did they start to search the Scriptures then? No. They had prepared themselves long ago. Before they even knew that such a scenario would take place, they were living the consecrated, set apart life.[3]

These men were not engaged in an admirable but optional lifestyle. They were actually following God's clear directive to all those who would follow Him, "Be holy, because I am holy" (1 Pet. 1:16). Holiness means to be set apart.[4]

In the closing words of the Old Testament, there is a prophecy regarding a future prophet. "See, I will send you the prophet Elijah before that great and dreadful day of the Lord comes. He will turn the hearts of the parents to their children, and the hearts of the children to their parents..." (Mal. 4:5–6). Like Elijah, he would one day come out of obscurity to challenge a nation trapped by the kingdom of this world. His message would bridge generational differences. These final words of Malachi resonated for four hundred long years—and then finally it happened.

A VOICE, NOT AN ECHO

Christ's disciples failed to comprehend the message of the Kingdom until Pentecost. How frustrating must that have been to Jesus? Imagine if you poured your life into a group of friends for over three years and they failed to comprehend much of what you were saying until after you had died!

There was one shining light, however. One man and only one man understood what was going on. He was not a prisoner of the culture. This man rejected social recognition and prestige. He was not interested in political solutions. His voice came from a foreign Kingdom. He was a man from the wilderness. Like Elijah, he had intentionally separated himself from the ambitions of this world. The food he ate was only appealing to the poor and starving. He failed to dress for success. He did not echo the passions and sentiments of the people. He was a foreign voice to a fallen culture.

The manner in which John the Baptist came into this world was both mysterious and prophetic. He possessed a sensitivity to God's presence even while in his mother's womb (see Luke 1:41). As John grew, he began to live a solitary lifestyle. This certainly did not get him the title of "Most Popular" or "Most Likely to Succeed" in the high school yearbook. However, at a critical moment in time, he arrived from the backside of the desert to prepare the way of the King and His Kingdom. His message became an irresistible force in the land. "From the days of John the Baptist until now, the kingdom of heaven has been subjected to violence..." (Matt. 11:12).

By word and lifestyle, John the Baptist attacked the temporal riches and pleasures of the prevailing culture. He constantly fought the religious system that had sold out to the world. He challenged the Roman Empire— the greatest military and political power that existed at that time. It would eventually cost him his life, but that was acceptable because of the greater spiritual good that would come.

He was just the type of person to prepare the world for the Messiah. He did not wear a crown or command an army. There is no record of John performing a miracle (see John 10:41). He did not write a book or a song. Yet when Jesus mentioned him, He bestowed on him great honor. "Truly I tell you, among those born of women there has not risen anyone greater than John the Baptist ..." (Matt. 11:11).

Eventually Jesus' ministry eclipsed John's. Rather than increasing his efforts to stay on top, John spoke of Jesus in a humble manner, "He must increase, but I must decrease" (John 3:30 KJV). John the Baptist had begun a battle against the powers of Babylon. Jesus would now finish it.

KEY TO SPIRITUAL TRANSFORMATION

We have seen revivals in every century in U. S. history. With this spiritual heritage, we may assume it will happen again. However, a major obstacle of any future revival is the unrelenting distractions that draw our hearts and minds away. Charles Finney witnessed incredible results in the nineteenth century, but he avoided holding revival meetings during the busy harvest season. Revival can overcome sin, the flesh, and the devil but not distractions. The last nationwide revival was the Jesus People Movement of the 1960s and '70s. However, this occurred before the Internet, cable TV, and video games were common in our homes.

Unless we intentionally disengage, we will never experience the deeper things of God. It doesn't matter how many times we repent or how often pastors pray together. Unless we change our way of life, we will never experience first-century Christianity. I believe this is why the spiritual outpourings in the West are small, transitory, and have minimal impact on the culture. We can no longer afford to assume that God will visit us mightily while we are holding on to the values of this world's system.

ONE SMALL STEP FOR MAN

A while back, my wife, Martha, and I sensed God leading us to take an additional step to disengage from Babylon. We decided to sell our home. This was no small issue. We had lived in our house longer than any other residence in our thirty-four years of marriage. We had a huge attic where we had stored old clothes, several sentimental items, and a lot of stuff. It would take considerable effort just to organize a move.

Despite the potential problems, I wanted to be objective. I had to admit we did not need this size home any longer. Martha and I were now empty nesters. Both our children, Molly and Dan, now had families of their own. We had also accumulated some debt, primarily because we had personally underwritten much of our ministry expenses the past few years. Nevertheless, the turning point came when God revealed to us how the American Dream had its roots in the kingdom of Babylon. We wanted our lives and lifestyle to demonstrate a commitment to the solution rather than the problem. If we wanted to experience the power of first-century Christianity, then we needed to live according to the values of the early Church.

I contacted a realtor who explained to us the current market conditions. Unfortunately, our suburb was the worst in the Twin Cities housing market. She told us that over seven hundred homes were available in our suburb alone, with half of those being foreclosures! This had driven the prices down and extended the length of time it would take to sell the home.

We knew this would be an incredible challenge. If we priced too high, we would not be able to sell. If we priced too low, we would not be able to pay our bills. We decided to price it higher than a "quick sale" recommendation and pray for divine intervention. It did not take God long. We sold the house in the same month we put it on the market. The sale price was very close to our asking price, and the proceeds would retire our debt.

When we sold our house, we felt prompted in our hearts to bless the buyers even though we had never met them. I patched and repainted where needed. I hired an expert to stretch the carpet. I left furniture and lawn equipment. We did a deep cleaning throughout. It took several days of hard work and a fair bit of expense, but we wanted to send a message. We wanted the spirit of giving rather than receiving to prevail over the transaction. We wanted them overwhelmed by good, and that is exactly what happened.

I have never before been to a real estate closing that felt like a worship service. The presence of God came down while we talked openly with our realtor about the goodness of God. The new buyers wept and gave us a gift in appreciation of the work we did to prepare their new home. It was awesome! It was such a contrast to the tension often associated with large financial transactions.

Our house sold on the same day that the venerable investment firm, Lehman Brothers, went bankrupt. Merrill Lynch, the largest brokerage house in the world at the time, was hastily taken-over by Bank of America on this same day. I sensed deliverance from a system that was obviously broken. As you know, the financial markets have continued to rock back and forth. The lending industry turned out to be a house of cards. As hard as this has been for our nation, I believe it potentially could lead us to a better spiritual condition.

I am not an economist or even a financial advisor. I am not suggesting we all sell our homes and live in the desert. Nevertheless, I do feel we have entered into a critical moment in our country's history. As a result, I believe we need to consider prayerfully getting rid of our extra stuff. We should focus on giving to others in need. We should get out of debt. We need to be free from Babylon's financial pressures.

THE DIVINE EXPERIMENT

What would happen if today we intentionally decided to set ourselves apart from the world's system to focus on the Kingdom of God? What would occur if we connected with other like-minded people? What would take place if we joined with other churches in our neighborhood to seek His Kingdom for an extended period? One spring we actually did this with several churches in the urban core.

During this extended time of seeking God, a number of Christians fasted from television, movies, and even the Internet. Others drank only water. Some churches cancelled all their weekly activities except Sunday mornings. People took intentional steps to minimize all distractions so they could set themselves apart for God.

Using a prayer guide provided for us by Fusion Ministries,[5] this "Divine Experiment" involved meeting for prayer each morning and evening except Sunday. The focus was repentance of our personal sins. We stationed a microphone at the front for anyone who wanted to share with the group. I was happy to see the pastors leading by example through their confession of sin.

About ten days into the experiment, a breakthrough occurred. First, the prayers became more desperate, and then faith seemed to rise. Finally, miracles began to occur. One of the female pastors went to a juvenile detention center and met with a dozen girls, and eleven of them prayed for salvation. Another participating church was conducting a service outside when six children from the neighborhood came by. They attended church before but had never responded to the gospel. That evening, all six gave their lives to Christ!

This church was located in a high-crime area and had a few drug houses on the same street. Despite desperate calls by many residents, the police were unsuccessful in stopping the drug traffic. During the Divine Experiment, we met several times at this church for prayer. After a few days, the host pastor discovered that the drug dealers had mysteriously abandoned their base of operations. Later, he contacted the local police and discovered that the crime around their church had dropped significantly. It had now become a place of peace.

A participant living in another section of the neighborhood was praying about a drug problem down the street from her house. Suddenly she heard a huge noise just outside. She looked out the window, and there were a dozen police officers, carrying shotguns, busting in the door of the house next to hers. There had been a major drug operation right beside her, and she only thought the threat was several houses away! God had brought deliverance to her, which changed her neighborhood.

A doctor informed one of the prayer participants that she had diabetes. Near the end of the three weeks, she went to her dietician. The doctor took some additional tests and discovered she no longer had the disease!

Another young woman received miraculous financial provision for her upcoming wedding. At one point, she wondered how she would be able to afford to fill up her car with gas when the tank began to fill up on its own. She also had been suffering from an illness for two years, but when she returned to the doctor, he discovered that her disease had disappeared.

Another female participant in the Divine Experiment had recent cataract surgery. She knew she had damaged retinas and would need an additional operation. Near the end of the three weeks of prayer, she contacted her ophthalmologist to arrange for the retinal surgery. In her pre-operative exam, the doctor discovered that there was nothing wrong with her retinas and the surgery was cancelled!

On the last weekend, the prayer focus of the Divine Experiment was on sexual immorality. During this weekend, local police and a federal agency busted a sex trafficking ring that had been running five brothels in Minneapolis and three in the surrounding suburbs. It was the largest bust of its kind in the history of Minnesota and became a national news story. What the press did not know was that the headquarters of this prostitution ring was across the parking lot from the church where we were praying! This evil existed behind the scenes, but God exposed and removed it from our midst.

We conducted a celebration service on the final evening. There was loud and spontaneous praise and worship as we celebrated God's presence and intervention. Denominational barriers had been broken, and racial barriers dissolved among participants. Our brokenness brought a deeper unity. There was a tremendous sense of victory.

There is a joy and freedom when we become detached from the Babylonian system. If we see our former priorities as harmful and dangerous, then it becomes a joy when they are removed.

> Long my imprisoned spirit lay,
> Fast bound in sin and nature's night;
> Thine eye diffused a quickening ray—
> I woke, the dungeon flamed with light;
> My chains fell off, my heart was free,
> I rose, went forth, and followed Thee.
> My chains fell off, my heart was free,
> I rose, went forth, and followed Thee.[6]

NOTES

1. Bob Marley, "Rasta man Chant," *Song Meanings*, http://www.songmeanings.net/songs/view/3530822107858526235/ (accessed 4/3/10).

2. John Mulinde, *Transforming Your World* (Jerusalem, Israel: Progressive Vision Publishing, 2005), 14–15.

3. Ibid., 17.

4. Hank Hanegraaff, "The Quest For Holiness," *Bible Answer Man*, http://www.oneplace.com/ministries/bible-answer-man/read/articles/quest-for-holiness-8355.html (accessed 12/4/10).

5. http://www.fusionministry.com.

6. Charles Wesley, "And Can It Be That I Should Gain?" (1738), http://www.cyberhymnal.org/htm/a/c/acanitbe.htm (accessed 1/20/11).

Chapter Notes

Chapter 16

THE WELL-DIGGER'S GUILD

*W*hat makes the desert beautiful is that somewhere it hides a well.
—ANTOINE DE SAINT-EXUPERY[1]

*D*rink water from your own cistern, running water from your own well.
—PROVERBS 5:15

atthew 12:43-45 provides us with some interesting insights in the operation of the dark side. "When an evil spirit comes out of a man, it goes through arid places seeking rest and does not find it. Then it says, 'I will return to the house I left.' When it arrives, it finds the house unoccupied, swept clean and put in order. Then it goes and takes with it seven other spirits more wicked than itself, and they go in and live there. And the final condition of that man is worse than the first." I believe the passage helps illustrate the danger of disengaging from Babylon but not replacing it with something better. Fortunately, God desires to refill our lives to the point of overflowing.

While evil spirits may prefer dry places, the Kingdom of God wants to fill us with life-giving water. Water is an incredibly important substance in our lives. Without water, you have no life. We use it to supply our body's internal needs, to clean ourselves, and to cool off on a hot summer's day. Our bodies are actually about two-thirds water, and doctors often recommend that we drink eight glasses per day. If we do not have enough in our system, we get headaches, experience weakness, and can even die of dehydration.

When Adam and Eve were created, they lived in a garden where rivers flowed (see Gen. 2:10–14). During the early days of human expansion, rivers, lakes, or abundant rainfall were necessary for survival, but one day something happened that changed the way we would live. While digging a deep hole, one of our common ancestors noticed water seeping into his good effort. He thought he knew the places where water was available but this was different; water was coming from a hole he had made in the ground.

Quickly, he ran home to his wife and children. When he returned with them, they discovered that water had completely filled the hole. Without realizing it, he had dug the first well. The kids immediately ran back to the house to get their swimming suits. Suddenly, everything was different. People could now move to regions beyond visible water sources. They were now free to go to even arid regions and survive because they could dig wells of life-giving water. The Bible says that Abraham obeyed God and went to a strange land. There, he dug a well (see Gen. 21:30). Later, he taught his son, Isaac, the art of well-digging (see Gen. 26:19–22).

With a good well, both humans and their livestock could survive. Often villages could flourish because of a community well. It only required daily visits with large pots to transfer the water back to each home. There was one problem, though; an enemy could attack the village and plug up the well. As a result, the village would no longer be sustainable unless they were able to clear the rocks and debris. The key defense for a community was having its water source securely guarded.

SPIRITUAL WELL-DIGGING

When we think of getting spiritual water, it is sometimes easy to imagine the Church as the "community well." Unfortunately, a community well of the spiritual type has a few disadvantages. These wells are not always open. In fact, the sanctuaries remain closed except for a few hours each week. Another problem occurs when the enemy attacks the community well and the life-giving water is blocked. Through sin, unforgiveness, or neglect, these wells may not produce enough water for everyone. Unless cleared, people will suffer from acute spiritual thirst. Spiritual death is even a possibility.

What is the solution? *I believe a critical component to spiritual survival is our ability to dig our own spiritual well.* In addition to the community well, we must make the places where we live a source of living water. This was the key to King David's success. When he was an unknown shepherd boy, he wrote and played music to the Lord. In his isolation, he built a well of intimacy with his God. What was the result? He received revelation, boldness, and strength for future times of crisis—first when confronting a lion, then a bear, and then finally the infamous giant, Goliath. With David's success, he brought honor to his God, obtained victory for his king, and won great favor with the people.

While in prison, Paul and Silas faced charges that could result in the death penalty. Rather than complaining about their living conditions or sending a prayer letter for deliverance, they dug a spiritual well in their prison cell. Despite their sore and wounded bodies, they entered into praise and worship that lasted far into the night. This attracted the presence of God, which had a supernatural impact. An earthquake resulted, and miraculously, all the chains fell off the prisoners.

The jailer quickly realized that this event could cost him his life if the prisoners were to escape. However, Paul and Silas did not intend to abandon the spiritual well they had just dug. They shared the gospel with the shaken jailer and his family, resulting in many becoming Christians. The jailer showed his appreciation by cleaning their wounds and ministering to their needs (see Acts 16:25–34). When they could have complained about their inability to visit the nearest community well, they chose rather to dig water where they were.

GROUNDWATER VERSUS RAINWATER

Originally, the earth was watered from beneath the ground (see Gen. 2:5–6). Rainwater only appeared after Noah built the Ark, and it was part of God's plan to cleanse the earth. With its initial appearance, rainwater did not create and sustain life. That task belonged to groundwater. Perhaps that is why the roots of trees go into the ground rather than toward the sky!

There are many benefits to the original design. A natural purification process occurs in ground water as it travels through the various levels of soil. Unlike rainwater, groundwater is naturally stored for future use. It also does not cause runoff problems or experience loss through evaporation like rainwater.

Today people are looking up for spiritual rainwater when they should be digging down for spiritual groundwater. These people run from conference to seminar with their rain buckets lifted high, hoping to get them filled. Unfortunately, regardless of the size of their buckets, they will soon run out again. They are seeking water designed to refresh them rather than sustain them. They may experience cleansing and renewal, but they will soon need additional water. Without learning to tap into the ground water, they are doomed to a life of intermittent showers rather than a consistent life-giving source.[2]

In 2006, the film *Faith like Potatoes* was released. Based on a true story, the challenge of faith occurred when the main character, Angus Buchan, planted a crop of potatoes during a time of drought. While everyone was praying for rain and looking to the skies, something else was happening deep within the soil. Without giving away the ending, I will say the Buchan family experienced divine intervention, but not in the way they were anticipating. Spiritual rain showers can be a great blessing but ground water is the key to our survival.

DIGGING OUR PERSONAL WELL

I had an incredible encounter with God in 1972 during the Jesus People Movement. I immediately began to live under a revival anointing. It was wonderful and exciting. But revival does strange things to people it touches. For me, I felt like Isaiah in the sixth chapter where he saw the Lord and declared, "I am ruined" (Isa. 6:5). That's often what revival does. It ruins you from the ordinary, nominal, and status quo religion. It's a good thing but can lead to dissatisfaction during seasons of dryness in the Church. If my only goal is to experience a large revival again, then I may face years of frustration and feelings of failure.

In over thirty years of ministry, I have faced seasons of barrenness. On one occasion, God brought our family into a valley where we faced obscurity and uncertainty. Fortunately, we discovered something unexpected in that valley—a well of life-giving water (see Gen. 26:19 AMP). During this time, we discovered a way to experience spiritual refreshing on a sustained basis.

This discovery happened during a spiritual retreat when the Lord impressed upon our team to increase our corporate prayer times. We first thought that we would add an extra prayer meeting in our weekly schedule, but God wanted more. We then discussed having two additional prayer meetings per week but still we felt we were missing the mark. In our restlessness, the Lord seemed to challenge our perspective on prayer. We discovered that He did not want us to treat prayer like an activity or event. He wanted us to possess a *prayer lifestyle* that would focus on knowing Him and fulfilling His desires. As a result, night after night, my family met in our house, where we played both intense and contemplative worship music and sought the face of God. We changed our television viewing habits and our use of free time. Soon God was visiting our personal well. It changed the very atmosphere of our home.

At first, I thought the grandchildren would be bored and uninterested, but they quickly became attracted to His presence. We started to experience spiritual dreams and visions. At times, we could sense angels in the room, and on one occasion, we clearly heard music coming down from heaven. My daughter received prophetic poems that we later put to music. Best of all, we were experiencing a constant flow of living water within our own home. This created a continual sense of His presence—even while we ate and slept. His Kingdom had come into our home, and it has not stopped for over five years!

We use music frequently, like the psalmist David and the early Church, to enter into His presence (see Eph. 5:19). One of the musical artists that we have grown to appreciate is Jason Upton. We seemed to identify naturally with his heart and passion. Then one day I discovered why. I came across a brief biography of Jason and noticed something quite remarkable about him and his wife, Rachel.

> During their time at Regent University, finishing their Masters of Divinity programs, they set up a worship room in their home where they regularly gathered with other worshipers to pray. It was during these times that they were convinced that the songs God was giving them during worship were not simply songs, but "keys that would open and shut doors in the spirit." Since that time Jason has been asked to sing and lead worship all over the country and the world.[3]

Ironically, God had also led Jason and his wife to build a spiritual well in their home. Because we lacked musical talent, we often chose music from several CDs and played them in different progressions for about an hour. Later, we learned how to create a playlist on our laptop and connect it to our sound system. We would then add to our music library through websites like Amazon or iTunes.

We also love to play various audio versions of the Scriptures. Now in mp3 format, audio Bibles have become inexpensive and easy to use. We know God honors His Word and we want to honor Him by filling our house with its eternal truths. We have times of personal study but we love an ongoing saturation of the atmosphere to gain broader spiritual insights.

Keys to Well-Digging

We desire God to live with us—not just visit us, but to stay with us. However, Jesus will only go where He is welcomed. "Here I am! I stand at the door and knock. If anyone hears my voice and opens the door, I will come in and eat with that person, and they with me" (Rev. 3:20). We must do more than give Him a one-time verbal invitation. Our lives need to express an ongoing desire for Him—not His blessings but Him. We want Him, we need Him, and we cannot live without Him.

Second, we need to remove anything that might make Him feel uncomfortable in our homes. Praise and worship music is not enough. We must come to Him with pure hearts. "Who may ascend the hill of the Lord? Who may stand in his holy place? He who has clean hands and a pure heart" (Ps. 24:3–4). Perhaps not everyone in the home is a Christian. If that is the case, try designating a particular room in the house as your spiritual well. Remember, Paul used the inner cell of a filthy prison!

Third, worship Him often. Welcome Him daily. Create an environment that honors Him. Focus on Him and His glorious Kingdom. This will lead you to more intimacy and spiritual revelation. Our hearts will cry out, "You are a garden fountain, a well of flowing water streaming down from Lebanon" (Song 4:15).

Finally, we need to realize that digging spiritual wells is not a performance-driven occupation. I have tasted the bitterness of self-effort too many times. If we are not careful, we can unconsciously slip into a religious ritual to achieve something for ourselves. To dig our spiritual wells, we need to lift our hearts simply and sincerely to the only source of living water. Success is found in Him, not a formula.

ROOT VALUE

Our worship and prayer times are often unpredictable. At times, we have sensed His presence immediately, and at other times, it has been more difficult. Occasionally, I felt I had failed when we did not have a tangible encounter with His presence. Nevertheless, God taught me something through this process. He said that some prayer times are full of fruit while others strengthen our spiritual root system.

The roots are a critical part of the plant, and God wanted us to value what we could not see. In other words, none of our prayer times have been a waste or failure! We may like to focus on the fruit, but we can miss the unlovely, unseen, yet critical root system of the plant.

What would happen to the plant if it had insufficient roots? It would dry up and die, of course. God wants us to be a complete and healthy plant, and not something that quickly fades away. The Bible tells us, "The righteous will flourish like a palm tree ..." (Ps. 92:12). This is significant because the palm tree has a more extensive root system than most trees. This gives them the ability to survive in dry seasons and remain steady when lashed by hurricane-force winds. "The righteous will never be uprooted, but the wicked will not remain in the land" (Prov. 10:30).

Many Christians dry up because of an inadequate root system. In an effort to demonstrate much fruit in a brief span of time, many have neglected what was necessary for sustainability. Our love will be tested to become stronger and more pure. It is vital that our roots go deep. Fruit is worthless if the plant cannot sustain itself; we need both. "Once more a remnant of the house of Judah *will take root below and bear fruit above*" (Isa. 37:31).

RELEASE OF THE BLACK HORSE

One night my daughter, Molly was getting herself ready for bed. Everything was silent, peaceful, and dark. Suddenly, she heard the sound of distant horse hooves. They started out faintly but then quickly became louder and louder. She knew whatever it was, it was coming closer and at a rapid pace. Molly opened her eyes and saw horses approaching her. She couldn't count how many, but there were just a few in number. Upon them were riders. They were not of flesh, but of spirit. Molly could not see the colors of the horses except for one, which was black.

Upon approaching her, the black horse and its rider stopped and looked at her very intensely. The horse was menacing and appeared possessed by a spirit. As it passed, she could feel the horse's breath upon her cheek. Molly began to cry out and tremble. The horse and rider then continued on their assigned mission with determined urgency. Her vision then expanded to where they were going. She saw them fly over the nations, and as they did, darkness consumed all that they passed over. The horse and rider brought mourning and woe, darkness, and ignorance to the land.

Molly began to cry out to the Lord, and as she did, her vision changed. She saw and heard the Lord crying out in agony, "My people are not ready. My people are not ready." He just repeated this over and over. Each time He cried out, it seemed as if His heart was breaking more. Molly then saw Him go throughout the different churches across the nations and the places where His people gathered. He started overturning their tables and chairs. As He did this, He cried out, "What you are doing is not going to prepare you for what is to come!" Molly had never felt the agony and desperation of the Lord as strong as that moment.

This open vision went on for over two hours. After it passed, the Lord directed her to His Word. He led Molly to Revelation 6, which describes the Four Horsemen of the Apocalypse. The black horse represents famine upon the earth. This is not only a physical famine but graver still, a spiritual famine.

In the passage, it speaks of wheat and barley that were once inexpensive but now their price has increased substantially. It was also now the case with our spiritual food. Where once we could easily preach, teach, prophesy, and heal, we will now have to pay a higher price to receive from the Lord. No longer will we be able to have God and the pleasures of this world, but we will have to spend more time with the God we profess to love.

In Revelation 6, no other horse and rider are given instructions but the black one. The Lord said to the rider, "Do not damage the oil and the wine." There is a difference between the roots of the wheat and barley compared to the olive tree and grapevine. Because of the wheat and barley's root system, they are picked once and then they die. They only last for a season and then the soil must be replanted. The olive tree and grapevine are different. When these plants are picked, they continue to live, even in dry seasons. They remain season after season. This is because their root systems are deeper and more substantial. I believe the Lord was saying that those whose roots are strong and deep in Him will be protected in the trials that are to come.

The black horse was not standing at the starting line. He was already running. The flag had been lowered, and he was off with only one thing on his mind—devastation. This is not something that Christians can ignore, rebuke, or cast back from where it came. It is already coming. Now is the time we must get others and ourselves ready.[4]

There will come a time when this world will be completely opposed to the Kingdom of God. We must be like Daniel and three Hebrew children, who dug their own spiritual wells while being held captive in Babylon. This is not to replace the Church but to populate the Church with overcoming saints. Rather than filled with parched believers who can barely make it from week to week, our churches will be filled with living vessels providing God's abundant source of life (see 1 Cor. 14:26). Christians will then thrive while others are struggling to survive a season of famine. With God, there will always be more than enough. Their surplus will serve as a spiritual oasis for many suffering from spiritual thirst in a kingdom void of life-giving water.

PRAYER

Lord, prepare me for the days ahead. Help me dig a spiritual well in my home. I want to learn how to draw from Your consistent groundwater so that I am not over dependent on intermittent rain showers. I want my roots to go deep so that I am a constant blessing rather than an inconsistent witness. May I have the unswerving passion of Daniel and the relentless ardor of the apostle Paul. I want to possess a prayer lifestyle that brings You pleasure and expands Your magnificent Kingdom. Amen.

NOTES

1. Antoine de Saint-Exupery, *Garden Digest*, http://www.gardendigest.com/water.htm (accessed 2/19/10).

2. Molly VanHeel, unpublished ministry notes, 3/10.

3. "Jason Upton," *LyricsFreak*, http://www.lyricsfreak.com/j/jason+upton/biography.html (accessed 11/18/10).

4. Molly VanHeel, "Bethany Urban Development News," 12/10.

Chapter Notes

Chapter 17

The Ruling Mandate

The supernatural potential of Christians laboring to establish the kingdom
of God together is so great that the reality of life in the typical church is both
depressing and comic by comparison.
—Daniel Taylor[1]

The secret of the kingdom of God has been given to you ...
—Mark 4:11

The book of Esther reflects the battle of two kingdoms. The storyline is like a heavyweight title fight. In one corner is Haman—rich, prideful, and hateful of God's people. He reflects the power of Babylon. In the other corner is Mordecai—wise, loving, faithful, and true. He reflects the Kingdom of God.

Initially, Esther fails to perceive the epic battle unfolding; she is unaware of the clash of kingdoms. When she finally hears the truth, she must then decide if she will respond with self-serving indifference or act with selfless courage. Esther could easily brush off the news of Haman's plot and focus on looking beautiful and acting like a queen. After all, to respond to the crisis will put her in great danger; she could possibly lose everything she possesses including her life. Fortunately, Esther chose to use her position to rule with honor. This produced national deliverance and the annihilation of the evil forces committed to her nation's destruction. Will the Western Church do the same?

Many churchgoers are unaware of the danger that exists because they are focusing on improving their position in a fallen culture. Others recognize the danger but are too centered on self-preservation to respond effectively to the crisis. The Church can try to save herself or join with God to save a nation. Perhaps by saving a nation, she will actually save herself. The choice is up to her. If she is to overcome, she must use all her God-given spiritual authority at every level of society. "And who knows but that you have come to royal position for such a time as this?" (Esth. 4:14).

Kingdom Rulership

Spiritual authority increases when we obey our mandate to rule. Jesus understood this principle and accepted His role as a King. He ruled over demonic powers, physical sicknesses, and religious fallacies. He then directed His disciples to do the same. Initially, many of Jesus' followers feared the power of Rome and the power of the religious establishment. Nevertheless, Christ wanted them to use their spiritual authority to rule.

The spiritual authority He gave them was impressive. "I have given you authority to trample on snakes and scorpions and to overcome all the power of the enemy; nothing will harm you" (Luke 10:19). "Truly I tell you, at the renewal of all things, when the Son of Man sits on his glorious throne, you who have followed me will also sit on twelve thrones, judging the twelve tribes of Israel" (Matt. 19:28). Later, the apostle Paul reinforced and expanded the message of ruling. "Do you not know that we will judge angels? How much more the things of this life!" (1 Cor. 6:3).

Reluctant to Rule

The principle of ruling goes all the way back to Creation. "Then God said, 'Let us make mankind in our image, in our likeness, so that they may rule over the fish of the sea and the birds in the sky, over the livestock and all the wild animals, and over all the creatures that move along the ground'" (Gen. 1:26). This passage reveals that God created man in His own image. This involved personality, intellect, creative powers, and the ability to make moral choices. We accept the first part of this passage, but for some strange reason, we avoid the second part. The Godhead not only made us in His image but also gave us a mandate to rule.

Early in the history of humanity, this calling was tested. In Genesis 3, we find a crafty serpent who offered something enticing to Eve with the hope she would violate God's command. We all know that she, along with Adam, gave in to the temptation and sin entered into the world. However, we have missed an important piece. Eve was given the commission to rule over the creatures "that move along the ground." Rather than ruling, she submitted to the serpent's suggestions and allowed him to rule over her. She abdicated her place in creation and suffered immeasurable grief for it. This failure to rule using her God-given authority was the reason sin entered the world.

Jonah also had a problem. God had directed him to go to Nineveh and preach against the city, but Jonah stubbornly refused. He desperately and foolishly did everything he could to avoid God's clear command. Finally, in the midst of a life-threatening storm at sea, Jonah realized his rebellious ways would never prevail. The ship's crew was desperate to find who was responsible for the storm before their ship was lost. Since Jonah was the only suspicious stranger on board, they demanded he give them some answers:

> "Tell us, who is responsible for making all this trouble for us? What kind of work do you do? Where do you come from? What is your country? From what people are you?" He answered, "I am a Hebrew and *I worship the Lord*, the God of heaven, who made the sea and the dry land" (Jonah 1:8–9).

Jonah spoke up and announced that he was a Hebrew and a worshipper of God. Jonah was not a fire-breathing prophet; he was a worshipper. But sometimes being a worshipper is not enough. Every citizen of God's Kingdom must rule in some capacity, and even worship cannot shield us from this responsibility.

God loved Jonah, but He also loved the people of Nineveh. This was no ordinary city. Years prior, Nimrod built Nineveh after he had built Babylon. He brought to Nineveh the same rebellious independent spirit (see Gen. 10:9–11). The rulership Nimrod demonstrated was evil and oppressive. God wanted to penetrate this kingdom of cruelty and replace it with His Kingdom of love. He wanted to set the people free from their past. It took a life-threatening storm and three days in the belly of a fish for Jonah to submit to God's way. A great revival came when Jonah was willing to walk in authority rather than run with indifference. Besides Eve and Jonah, there were others who neglected to rule. God rebuked the high priest Eli for failing to rule over his sons (see 1 Sam. 3:12–13). In Revelation, Jesus rebuked the church in Thyatira for tolerating a controlling spirit, which was leading His people astray (see Rev. 2:20).

Today, our failure to properly rule has continued to create enormous problems in the world and in the Church. On one hand, there are those who take this mandate to rule and use it to control the lives of others for personal benefit and gain. Abusive parents, controlling bosses, and some ministry leaders are in this category. Many sincere Christians have suffered years of spiritual abuse in various churches and ministries. As great of a problem as this is, the opposite may even be worse. Most people today are abdicating their responsibility to rule both outside and inside the Church. In our battle against Babylon, we must rule or be ruled.

In most Western homes, children fight parents for control of the home and often prevail. "Skinny kids terrorize my people. Silly girls bully them around ..." (see Isa. 3:12 MSG). This has created much dysfunction and pain. In our effort to be sensitive and tolerant, many parents have enabled irresponsible behavior in their children. A lack of boundaries and discipline reveals a lack of proper rulership.

Surprisingly, some homes struggle with even ruling their own pets. There are cable television programs that focus on this problem. One in particular is focused on overweight pets (generally dogs) and the struggle to get them to a proper weight so they will enjoy a normal, happy life. The difficulty is not so much with the pet as it is with the owners, who often suffer from misguided compassion. Even when the pet regains their health through a strict regime of diet and exercise, they quickly return to obesity because of the owners' reluctance to rule over their pets' appetites.

THE SPIES' DEMISE

Proper rulership is very important to God. Why did the Children of Israel have to wander in the wilderness for forty years? Was it because they bowed down to a golden calf? Was it because of their constant complaining? Was it because of their rebellion against Moses' leadership? No. They were guilty of all these things, yet these sins failed to bring a forty-year sentence upon them. Only one thing caused that terrible consequence—their unwillingness to rule over the Promised Land after the report from the twelve spies. What was so terrible about their reluctance? Like Jonah, it reflected indifference on establishing the Kingdom of God where it was needed most.

The Children of Israel were seriously jeopardizing their opportunity to live in their own land separated from the oppressive power of Egypt. In addition, they were preventing the fulfillment of the covenant promise first given to their obedient forefather, Abraham. Finally, their unwillingness to rule over the Promised Land was a refusal to endorse God's redemptive plan for all humanity. The Promised Land was the location where Christ would one day be born. This Christ was the only hope for the world, but the Children of Israel were uninterested in spiritual destiny, God's covenant, or the future of the human race. They chose to focus on the size of their enemies rather than the power of their God and His Kingdom.

FIRST WE YIELD, THEN WE WIELD

Rulership is critical, but it needs to be exercised from a humble spirit and a servant's heart. In Exodus 17:9, Joshua first appears in the Scriptures leading the Israelite army against the Amalekites. Despite Joshua's skill and bravery, the fight was not going well. From the top of a bordering hill, Moses witnessed something indistinguishable by others. He saw someone other than brave Joshua trying to defeat the Amalekites. He saw himself. Yes, I believe Moses saw a reflection of himself years ago trying to kill an

Egyptian to free his fellow Hebrew slaves. He was witnessing once again the futility of doing God's work man's way. He saw, in zealous Joshua, a warrior who lacked the understanding of how the Kingdom of God operates. Moses immediately sought the Lord for help. As long as Moses was able to raise his staff, the battle went favorably, but if he faltered, the Amalekites prevailed. The outcome of the battle that day was more dependent on Moses than Joshua because he understood the ways of God's Kingdom.

God had previously taught Moses His ways by breaking his self-effort, pride, and independence in a wilderness. As Moses went to the School of God Dependency in the desert of Midian for forty years, so Joshua would go through forty years in another wilderness. It takes time to make a man or woman of God. The famous author and intercessor E. M. Bounds said that it takes twenty years to make a preacher.[2] Moses saw the need for a change in Joshua and made him his personal aid and caretaker of the Tabernacle. In a position of service and submission, Joshua would learn to worship and minister in the presence of the Lord. The resulting spiritual development would be essential for conquering the Promised Land.

After forty years, Moses died and Joshua became the leader of the Children of Israel. Now, after learning the importance of intimacy with God and disengagement from the world, Joshua needed to pick up his sword again. The destiny of the land needed to be reclaimed, and God had just the man to do it.

I HAVE NOW COME

As Joshua and his army approached Jericho, a surprising visitor met him on the road. This warrior confronted Joshua with a drawn sword. He was armed and ready to fight. Joshua asked, "'Are you for us or for our enemies?'

'Neither,' he replied, 'but as commander of the army of the LORD *I have now come*'" (Josh. 5:13-14). His answer was a vivid reminder that the Lord does not represent or fight for any Kingdom but His own. This will never change.

The warrior's declaration *"I have now come"* also reminds me of a story I heard several years ago. There was a pastor who constantly prayed, "Lord, send revival; send revival." But nothing changed. He grew more desperate, "Lord, send revival; send revival." But still no answer. Finally, as he continued to cry out, the Lord spoke something so simple yet so profound, "I don't send revival, *I come!*"

For God to come, we must consider what happened before Joshua's encounter. God had just renewed His covenant with His people at Gilgal. Through forming an altar and reinstituting circumcision, the Children of Israel had reestablished their love commitment to the Lord. As they did, the Lord declared, "Today I have rolled away the reproach of Egypt from you" (Josh. 5:9). This declaration revealed that the Hebrews had finally disengaged from the world's system. They also celebrated the Passover to remember the Lord's faithfulness. They were now armed for battle and anxious to fulfill their God-given mandate to take the land.

I have hungered for a culture-changing move of God since experiencing it in 1972. At times, this burden has overwhelmed and consumed me. I know it is God's desire to come to us. I know He has come to other parts of the world. I know what brought the Lord to Joshua and the Children of Israel applies to us today. We may think we have been waiting for Him but actually, He has been waiting for us. Waiting for our whole hearts. Waiting for us to let go of this world. Waiting for us to fulfill our mandate to rule.

On Earth as It Is in Heaven

Joshua successfully penetrated Canaan and replaced the existing culture with the Kingdom of God. I believe his ministry assignment contains a prophetic call to the Church. "If we don't deliberately reach out and possess the land, the land will possess us."[3] Fortunately, God has given us spiritual weapons and giftings to take the land.

The Lord established a five-fold ministry strategy in the New Testament (see Eph. 4:11). One of these gifts is particularly important in ruling the land. When we think of an apostle, we conjure up thoughts of an incredibly gifted man or woman of God. We often picture them overseeing many other Christian leaders. This may be true in many cases, but let me suggest another definition of an apostle given by John Mulinde.

They work for territory. The apostles are father figures, foundation builders, pathfinders, and pioneers. They are people who see territory, do not limit themselves to boundaries in theologically different church movements, but rather say, "We want to claim our nation or community." They are people who will have the heart to recognize God's soldiers in any denomination. They will have humility to forge bridges across denominational barriers and have no competitive spirit.[4]

If we use this definition, then Joshua was an apostle. By what we have discussed earlier, Jesus certainly fulfilled the office of an apostle. The Lion of Judah came in the Spirit of a lamb to conquer all the kingdoms of man. He then taught His disciples to do the same (see Matt. 28:19; Acts 17:26–27). This is our spiritual mandate and destiny!

THE KINGDOM IN OUR NATIONS

Several years ago in Uganda, the Church prayed that God would deliver them from the oppressive rule of their dictator. He eventually left, but then another tyrant came into power. Again, the Church prayed, and he was dethroned. Soon after, an unprecedented outbreak of AIDS occurred. The Church began to get discouraged because one crisis followed another. Then the Lord spoke:

> You have suffered a lot but have not learned much out of it. Up until now, you still look at flesh and blood as your enemy and that is why you focus on crises and problems. When you pray against problems, they will go, and others will come. If you pray for my purposes, as my purposes are being fulfilled, the land will change and the kingdom of God will be manifest. Choose today to change the focus of your prayers, from concentrating on problems to concentrating on my purposes.[5]

This revelation changed the direction and focus of the Church's intercession.

> As we sought the Lord, He began to speak, turning our attention away from the crisis, to pray for the destiny of the nation. He was revealing to us that He has a destiny and purpose for every single nation of the earth,

and that the ultimate working of the kingdom of God on the earth, is when the nations come to fullness.[6]

It is up to us to contend for God's will to be done in our nation as it is in heaven. I can see of no greater use of our lives than to aim to fulfill His purposes on earth.

THE KINGDOM IN OUR COMMUNITIES

We also need a Kingdom-expanding vision for the community where we live. We need to challenge our society's fallen values and reach out, in love, to those facing frustration and fear. We need to see a fresh outpouring of miracles, signs, and wonders—to expand the Kingdom of God rather than to promote our organizations or ourselves.

We must see past the four walls of our churches and see our community as our parish. We must also recognize that no one pastor, church, or ministry will be able to release Kingdom transformation in our community alone. It must be a collaborative effort. In a spirit of humility, we need to forge partnerships and alliances with other Kingdom builders.

We must share more than the message of salvation to our neighbors and co-workers. God has given us a Kingdom and He wants others to know about this better way of life. We need to go where Jesus would go and share the message He would constantly teach.

THE KINGDOM IN OUR LIVES

The Ark of the Covenant contained God's presence. Everywhere it went, things changed. It conquered opposing kingdoms, causing their gods to fall (see 1 Sam. 5:3–4). It also brought great blessing to those aligned with God's Kingdom (see 2 Sam. 6:11–12). Like the Ark of the Covenant, our lives are to be carriers of His presence. Things should change everywhere we go. The power of His Kingdom will affect those we know and meet.

We are called to be citizens of an eternal, unchanging Kingdom. Therefore, resignation to the power of an inferior kingdom is unacceptable. Coexistence of two kingdoms is no longer an option. Our lives must represent the penetrating and replacing Kingdom. My barber has met Christ, along with my insurance agent, real estate agent, and home security specialist. If the Kingdom is what the Bible says it is, then it must touch every area of our lives.

FOR THE HONOR OF HIS NAME

God said, "Those who honor me I will honor" (1 Sam. 2:30). King David faced many hardships but always desired to uphold God's honor. This was the secret of his success against Goliath. "David said to the Philistine, 'You come against me with sword and spear and javelin, but I come against you in the name of the Lord Almighty, the God of the armies of Israel, whom you have defied'" (1 Sam. 17:45).

Another time David told the prophet Nathan that it was wrong for the king to enjoy "a house of cedar, while the ark of God remains in a tent" (2 Sam. 7:2). David was not trying to get something from God. His heart deeply desired God's honor and blessing. As a result, God generously responded to David's concern. Imagine if God's reputation and glory were our primary concern. Imagine if His honor and Kingdom purposes constantly fueled our prayers.

In the book of Haggai, God pointed out that the sin of the Children of Israel was that they were more interested in their own welfare than God's, "'You expected much, but see, it turned out to be little. What you brought home, I blew away. Why?' declares the Lord Almighty. 'Because of my house, which remains a ruin, while each of you is busy with your own house'" (Hag. 1:9). If we focus on our own safety and prosperity, we will face disappointments and frustrations, but if we focus on His purposes, even our prayers will begin to change.

- Rather than, "God, meet our financial needs," we would pray, "God, release resources so Your Kingdom may expand without limitations."

- Rather than, "God, deliver us from this problem," we would pray, "God, make our lives a living testimony of Your power and love. May Your will be done with signs and wonders for Your honor and praise" (see Acts 4:29–30).

- Rather than asking God for strength to be a good Christian, we would pray, "May the dreams You have held for our lives come to pass. May we become the reward of Your sufferings."

- Rather than, "God, send revival to our city so drugs, crime, and poverty will cease," we would cry out, "Rend the heavens and come down for the glory of Your name and the furtherance of Your Kingdom. May our city fulfill the destiny You have desired for it."

PRAYER

Lord, at this critical time in earth's history, we need a culture-changing spiritual reformation. May it come with such power that it transforms our families, communities, and nations. We ask this for Your sake, not ours. For too long we have been indifferent to Your plans and reluctant to rule as You have commanded. Grant us the grace to rise with You at such a time as this. We want Your name to be honored and Your Kingdom purposes fulfilled. We offer ourselves and commit our hearts to this great and glorious cause. Lead on, oh King Eternal!

NOTES

1.   Daniel Taylor, *The Myth of Certainty* (Grand Rapids, MI: Zondervan Publishing House, 1992), 108.

2.   Leonard Ravenhill, *Why Revival Tarries* (Zachery, LA: Fires of Revival Publishers, 1971), 106.

3.   John Mulinde, *Transforming Your World* (Jerusalem, Israel: Progressive Vision Publishing, 2005), 77.

4.   Ibid., 111–12.

5.   Ibid., 30.

6.   Ibid., 87.

Chapter Notes

Chapter 18

MARCH OF THE LOYAL MINIONS

The readiest way to escape from our sufferings is,
to be willing they should endure as long as God pleases.
—JOHN WESLEY[1]

They triumphed over him by the blood of the Lamb
and by the word of their testimony ...
—REVELATION 12:11

A number of years ago, I was able to take my father trout fishing on the Little Red River in Arkansas. This was his first experience catching these beautiful and intelligent fish. Rainbow and brown trout are great fighters and often make spectacular jumps when hooked. However, they are also particularly challenging to catch. They require a very light line that is invisible to their sensitive eyes. The drag on the reel must also be light to reduce the chance of breaking the line on a prized lunker (trout exceeding four pounds).

On this particular day, we had enjoyed a successful morning upstream catching some "keepers." We began to settle into a warm, albeit quiet, afternoon near a bend in the river. We had some lines in the water, but without any bites, I began to drift off to sleep.

Suddenly, a loud *bang* coming from the center of our small aluminum boat jolted me awake. I anxiously looked around for the source and was shocked to see my fishing pole sinking out of sight into the dark, cold current.

I was staring at my dad in disbelief when suddenly a lunker-size rainbow trout jumped about fifty feet from our boat. Could this trophy-size trout be responsible for the loss of my fish pole? It appeared to be, but there was very little we could to about it. Our only chance was to salvage my fishing pole, but that seemed impossible in the turbulent frigid river.

Then my dad shocked me with an improbable solution. He happened to be carrying a lure in his tackle box that was notorious for getting stuck on rocks and debris. Perhaps in this case, we could use it to our advantage by snagging my fishing pole or its line at the bottom of the river. He cast a few times without any luck. I was thinking our chances were slim when all of a sudden he exclaimed, "I've got something! I think it is your line!" As he slowly reeled in, the pressure on the line frightened the trout, causing it to jump from the watery depths in an effort to shake the hook again.

Finally, we were able to bring my dad's lure to the surface, and sure enough, there was my line extended over one of the hooks. I immediately grabbed it, knowing one end went to the fish and the other to my pole. We then maneuvered the boat so that we were directly above the sunken fishing pole. I nervously pulled on the line, but surprisingly, it would not budge—the fish pole had become stuck on the bottom of the river! Because we were using very light line, I was so afraid that my efforts to dislodge the pole would break the line. With still no success, I had to increase the pull on the line to the breaking point. Suddenly, the line gave. I thought, *Is the pole free or has the line broken?* Quickly, I pulled in the line, and after a few anxious moments—up came my fishing pole!

I then rapidly reeled in the loose line until I could finally feel the full weight of the fish. The fish fought long and hard, but eventually we pulled it up to the side of the boat. It was the biggest lunker trout I had ever seen. My dad reached over and … successfully netted him!

I will never forget the experience. It was special because it was just my dad and me. It was also special because my dad would not let me give up. I learned an important lesson in perseverance. It is not enough to get a hold of something good; it takes determination to gain the prize. God gives strength to those who remain steady despite the outward circumstances. "Let us run with perseverance the race marked out for us" (Heb.12:1b).

THE POWER OF PERSISTENCE

Jesus taught His disciples to pray, but He also taught them to be persistent in their prayers.

> Then he said, "Imagine what would happen if you went to a friend in the middle of the night and said, 'Friend, lend me three loaves of bread. An old friend traveling through just showed up, and I don't have a thing on hand.' The friend answers from his bed, 'Don't bother me. The door's locked; my children are all down for the night; I can't get up to give you anything.' But let me tell you, even if he won't get up because he's a friend, if you stand your ground, knocking and waking all the neighbors, he'll finally get up and get you whatever you need" (Luke 11:5–8 MSG).

To be Christ's friend is incredibly important, but this parable reveals that friendship alone is not always sufficient for answered prayer. He wants us to learn the value of being persistent as well as being His friend.

Another time, Jesus told a parable about a woman who needed help with an adversary. She appealed to a judge whom she knew could help. The judge ignored her requests for a time but eventually answered her persistent appeal for justice. "And will not God bring about *justice* for his chosen ones, who cry out to him day and night? Will he keep putting them off? I tell you, he will see that they get *justice*, and quickly. However, when the Son of Man comes, will he find faith on the earth?" (Luke 18:7–8). Like this persistent woman, we need to contend for God's justice. "Will not the Judge of all the earth do right?" (Gen. 18:25).

STAIRWAY TO HEAVEN

Jacob left Beersheba and set out for Haran. When he reached a certain place, he stopped for the night because the sun had set. Taking one of the stones there, he put it under his head and lay down to sleep. He had a dream in which he saw a stairway resting on the earth, with its top reaching to heaven, and the angels of God were ascending and descending on it (Gen 28:10–12).

One day my wife, during a prayer meeting, saw a similar staircase that went to heaven. At the top of the stairs, the Lord stood. Martha knew she would not be able to get to Him without putting forth the effort to climb the stairs. Some Christians see God at a distance and are content with their position. Others are willing to get closer but look for the nearest escalator or elevator.

I remember during the Jesus People Movement, many engaged in "revival praying." It was earnest, desperate, and loud. Although the flesh may try to imitate, sincere believers who pray with their hearts and minds fully engaged will rise to heavenly communion more frequently.

Jacob only saw a stairway to heaven. Stairways take effort. "You will seek me and find me when you seek me with all your heart" (Jer. 29:13). "Let us, therefore, make every effort to enter that rest…" (Heb. 4:11). "The effective, fervent prayer of a righteous man avails much" (James 5:16 NKJV).

CONTENDER OR PRETENDER

Citizens of the Kingdom must learn how to contend for spiritual breakthroughs. When we face a crisis beyond our ability to change, we naturally call upon the Lord for help. Often with heartfelt prayers, there comes a sense of His presence and an assurance that He has heard us. We then begin to walk in confidence that God has everything under control. However, after a while, we may notice no appreciable change and possibly matters getting worse. It is then that we must recognize the importance of contending for the fulfillment of the answer. It is imprudent to say we are trusting God and then fall into the trap of passivity.

Beyond a realization that He has heard us, often we must battle for a change in circumstances. Revelation is not equivalent to fulfillment. Many receive revelation but fail to see the fulfillment because they took a passive approach afterward. Elijah received revelation regarding rain, but nothing happened until he sought God diligently for it. Elisha knew that God had given the Shunammite woman a son, but he had to contend for her son's recovery. Daniel was given revelation regarding the future of Israel, but he had to contend for its fulfillment. His prayers were immediately heard, but for twenty-one days, he faced stiff demonic resistance (see Dan. 10:12–14). His persistence in prayer secured the needed breakthrough.

In a time of crisis, Jacob was rewarded because he was willing to wrestle for a divine intervention. "Jacob said, 'I'm not letting you go 'til you bless me.' The man said, 'What's your name?' He answered, 'Jacob.' The man said, 'But no longer. Your name is no longer Jacob. From now on it's Israel (God-Wrestler); *you've wrestled with God and you've come through*'" (Gen. 32:26–28 MSG).

PETITIONS THAT OVERCOME OPPOSITION

In 1 Samuel 7, we find that the Philistines were oppressing the Children of Israel. They cried out to the Lord, and He sent the prophet Samuel with instructions for deliverance. They complied by putting away their gods, fasting, and confessing their sins. Ironically, the Philistines responded by mustering their powerful army to attack them. This was not exactly the deliverance they were looking for! It created a panic in Israel, and they begged Samuel to petition the Lord on their behalf. Samuel did so, and a miraculous deliverance subsequently occurred.

In 2 Kings 19, we find King Hezekiah under siege in Jerusalem. The Assyrian army had intimidated the people with threats and had blasphemed the Lord. As the nation's leadership sought the Lord, Isaiah the prophet provided the king with the words he was hoping to hear. He said to Hezekiah, "Don't be upset by what you've heard, all those words the servants of the Assyrian king have used to mock me. I personally will take care of him" (Isa. 37:6–7 MSG). This greatly improved King Hezekiah's outlook on the situation, but something happened next that staggered him. Hezekiah received a letter from Sennacherib, king of Assyria, demanding an immediate surrender of Jerusalem. This threat was more ominous and vicious than anything received previously.

King Hezekiah was so broken over the letter that he went to the temple and laid it out before the Lord. This was terrible news rather than the good news he was expecting. He cried to the Lord and said, "Give ear, Lord, and hear; open your eyes, Lord, and see; listen to the words Sennacherib has sent to ridicule the living God" (Isa. 37:17). Hezekiah reminded God that things were not going well, even though the Lord had promised victory. He appealed to God's justice and honor.

God responded by directing Isaiah to send a message to Hezekiah that the city would endure and the Assyrian king would leave. That night the angel of the Lord killed one hundred eight-five thousand Assyrian soldiers. Sennacherib broke camp and returned home.

"But If Not"

The Babylonian captivity was one of the darkest moments in Israel's history. For many years, God's prophets had warned the people, but they were unwilling to repent. Now the unthinkable had occurred; they were taken into captivity by the Babylonian army. As a result, they lost their freedom, their homeland, and much of their culture. In the midst of their loss, three young men had remained committed to follow the God of their fathers. Even in a foreign land, they had remained steadfast. They had chosen to seek the Lord privately and earnestly.

Their commitment eventually created a showdown between two belief systems. An immense golden image was constructed, and the king of Babylon commanded everyone to bow to it. When the three young men refused, King Nebuchadnezzar was publically humiliated and became enraged. Their sentence was to be swift and severe—cast alive into a fiery furnace. Facing such a fate, the three young men were undaunted in their commitment to a superior Kingdom. Their dedication to God stood in sharp opposition to the most powerful kingdom in the world.

> O Nebuchadnez'zar, we have no need to answer you in this matter. If it be so, our God whom we serve is able to deliver us from the burning fiery furnace; and he will deliver us out of your hand, O king. *But if not*, be it known to you, O king, that we will not serve your gods or worship the golden image which you have set up (Dan. 3:16–18 RSV).

Shadrach, Meshach, and Abednego boldly defied a corrupt culture and its narcistic emperor with boldness and resolve. The result? God delivered them that day, and the king humbled himself before their God (see Dan. 3:28–29).

This is an account of overcoming all odds. We love the story because we would like to make such an impact in this world, but there is a problem. We have failed to understand their response to the king's demand. As we look closely, we find their confidence in the outcome to be not as certain as we would like to assume. The threat of death was real to them, and the uncertainty of the outcome was equally real. These three young men were willing to make the ultimate sacrifice to remain faithful to God's Kingdom. They took a stand for God but included the poignant phrase, *"But if not."*

Today, there is a Christian culture that assumes people will escape injury or harm if they do the right thing. There is an expectation of seeing success if a prescribed order of conduct is followed, but is this scriptural? Hebrews 11 paints a different story. Shadrach, Meshach, and Abednego escaped the fiery furnace, while others paid the ultimate price for their commitment to the King and His Kingdom.

THE PRICE OF FAITHFULNESS

We have faced many challenges and opportunities in our cross-cultural urban ministry. The focus has always been serving the poor and the disenfranchised. This includes least-reached immigrant groups, neglected children, and homeless drug addicts. The spiritual warfare has been real and intense, but so are the potential rewards.

After we started the ministry, I quickly saw an increase in demonic attacks on our team. Staff members were compiling a history of car breakdowns, vehicle accidents, and health problems soon after joining our ministry. Those who worked as volunteers and supporters also suffered. This appeared to be more than coincidence. The scenario became too familiar—those who became involved with us faced increased hardships. I sometimes felt sorry for those called to work with us.

Establishing God's Kingdom in a culture dominated by Babylonian values is going to cost something. Holding onto God and His promises often results in some painful experiences. Os Guinness explains the potential cost of faithfulness to God's Kingdom:

> The first cost of faithfulness is *a sense of maladjustment*. When society is increasingly godless and the church increasingly corrupt, faithfulness carries a price: the man or woman who lives by faith does not fit in ...
>
> The second cost of faithfulness is *a sense of impatience*. For when society becomes godless and the church corrupt, the forward purposes of God appear to be bogged down and obstructed, and the person who lives by faith feels the frustration ... And their natural cry is "How long, O Lord?" ...
>
> The third cost of faithfulness is *a sense of failure*. For when society becomes godless and the church corrupt, the prospects of good people succeeding are significantly dimmed and the temptation to feel a failure is ever-present ...
>
> Any sense of failure, then, is maddening, for a calling is a project like any venture. And after all, who likes to fail at any task we take on? Yet the truth is that in certain situations and periods of history, failure is only to be expected ...
>
> In King David's time, or even later in the reign of good kings such as Hezekiah and Josiah, a man of character with ambition might easily have risen to the top of society. But in the grim days of King Zedekiah, evil rather than goodness was fashionable, so there was little scope for good men or women to succeed. The price of faithfulness was apparent failure.[2]

THE TESTING OF OUR FAITH

One night we conducted a prayer vigil in the urban core. It involved several local churches and ministries. We had extensive worship, corporate prayer, and a prayer walk through a dangerous neighborhood. It was strategic intercession for our troubled community. As we concluded shortly after midnight, a young woman who was the prayer coordinator for one of the churches went out to her car. She immediately discovered that her new computer, containing all the prayer records of their church, had been stolen from her car. At 5:00 AM, the host church's pastor received a call from their security company. Apparently, someone had just broken into the church. The police confirmed the break in and the subsequent damage.

As I was receiving this news in my home the next day, I heard a weak cry for help from my wife in the adjacent room. I quickly responded, only to find her fainting and falling down the steps. She sustained minor injuries, including a strong blow to her head.

Later that day, the hosting pastor contacted me again. That morning, his car was broken into at his church. This had not happened in twenty years. They smashed the passenger side window, damaged the body, and stole hundreds of dollars worth of equipment. We always hope for results we experienced during the "Divine Experiment," but is that the only acceptable outcome? Is suffering loss always an indication of failure? Is there no acceptable place for suffering for His Kingdom's sake?

THE BLESSING OF SUFFERING

Prior to Pentecost, the disciples were hesitant to suffer for their faith. This led to Peter's denial and their collective hiding from the religious authorities. After Pentecost, we see a completely different attitude toward suffering. It was not a sign of failure any longer but a badge of honor. "They called the apostles in and had them flogged. Then they ordered them to stop speaking in the name of Jesus, and let them go. The apostles left the Sanhedrin, rejoicing because they had been counted worthy of suffering disgrace for the Name" (Acts 5:40–41).

They also declined to focus on deliverance and favor from those opposing them. Rather they prayed, "Lord, consider their threats and enable your servants to speak your word with great boldness" (Acts 4:29). The early Church displayed a genuine joy in the midst of their suffering. They declined to look back, and they refused to look down. They embraced Christ's Kingdom lifestyle, which still challenges us today.

Do you see what this means — all these pioneers who blazed the way, all these veterans cheering us on? It means we'd better get on with it. Strip down, start running — and never quit! No extra spiritual fat, no parasitic sins. Keep your eyes on Jesus, who both began and finished this race we're in. Study how he did it. Because he never lost sight of where he was headed — that exhilarating finish in and with God — he could put up with anything along the way: cross, shame, whatever. And now he's there, in the place of honor, right alongside God. When you find yourselves flagging in your faith, go over that story again, item by item, that long litany of hostility he plowed through. That will shoot adrenaline into your souls! (Heb. 12:1-3 MSG).

The present underground Church in China has embraced this admonition. Their prayer is for God to give them stronger backs rather than lighter loads. In struggling countries where poverty and bloodshed are commonplace, we often find saints of God who possess thick skins but soft hearts. In the West, where prosperity and self-indulgence rule, we often find lukewarm believers with thin skins and hard hearts. Too many Christians today want to overlook the strength of character that suffering will develop. They anxiously await the rapture while in a weakened spiritual condition.

The apostle Paul suffered severely because of his faith, yet he refused to look at his sufferings negatively but rather as a positive means of expanding God's Kingdom.

> Now I want you to know, brothers and sisters, that what has happened to me has actually served to advance the gospel. As a result, it has become clear throughout the whole palace guard and to everyone else that I am in chains for Christ. And because of my chains, most of the brothers and sisters have been confident in the Lord and dare all the more to proclaim the gospel without fear (Phil. 1:12–14).

Paul often addressed the subject of suffering in his letters and encouraged believers to keep it in perspective. "Not that the troubles should come as any surprise to you. You've always known that we're in for this kind of thing. It's part of our calling ..." (1 Thess. 3:3 MSG). He used his life as an example, "We also glory in our sufferings, because we know that suffering produces perseverance" (Rom 5:3). He was concerned that the new followers might waste their sorrows. Paul believed that suffering prepares believers for God's Kingdom (see 2 Thess. 1:5). He even encouraged Timothy to join with him in suffering for the gospel (see 2 Tim. 1:8). However, this was not just a physical suffering. Paul was also addressing suffering that comes through the loss of our positions, ambitions, and desires.

GOD'S BUILDING BLOCKS

Our suffering often produces the building blocks God needs to create something significant. Unlike common construction methods, He uses materials that many would perceive as worthless or impractical. Two of these extraordinary materials are ashes and tears. Ashes are the charred remains of what once was but is no more—the empty reminders of loss and death. A life, a love, a vision, and a dream are all susceptible to death. Tears are often the internal gushing of an open wound—the painful bleeding of a broken heart.

Throughout the Scriptures, we see the Lord responding to those with ashes on their heads and tears in their eyes. When Christ walked the earth, He was constantly attracted to those who were suffering. The sentiments of the culture suggested they had failed, but Jesus saw the treasure buried deep within. They possessed something He could use to rebuild the world.

God reacts with passion for those whose hearts are completely His. They will arise from the ashes of suffering and the tears of disappointment. They will shine like the dawn because their God will not allow them to be ashamed. He is their eternal defender, lover, and friend.

One time Jesus as ked my daughter a compelling question. "Molly, if you could bring one thing with you to Heaven, what would you bring?"

She softly responded to Him, "I know you have spoken in your Word that you will wipe away every tear, but if it's not too much to ask, can I keep mine? I cannot worship you without them. My tears remind me of where you have taken me from and where you are taking me to. They are my silent 'I love yous'."

Jesus then spoke back and said, "I will let you keep them, if I can keep mine." At that moment she realized that His tears are His silent "I love yous" too.

Revelation 21 states that there will be no more death, mourning, crying (grief[3]), or pain. However, it says He will wipe away our tears. Could this passage reveal that He tenderly touches our tears of love as our tears of grief have passed away?

ALL FOR LOVE

In the ancient Persian Empire, King Xerxes faced a dilemma. He had thrown a lavish party and commanded his wife to join him. However,

Queen Vashti refused to come because she was entertaining her own guests (see Est. 1:10–2:4). She was preoccupied with her own interests, to the detriment of the king's desires. The penalty for her disrespect and indifference was simple but painful; she was replaced. The King of kings is also looking for those who will put Him and His Kingdom first—those who will come when He calls and stay as long as He desires. "Do not be in a hurry to leave the king's presence" (Eccl. 8:3).

The Bride of Christ will someday stand spotless and pure. Her impressive beauty will only be eclipsed by her passion to fulfill the Bridegroom's desires. Like the angels, her heart will be completely aligned with His plans and purposes. No secondary agendas. No other kingdoms. No other desires. Am I being too idealistic? Can this only happen in heaven? Or could this be our spiritual destiny on earth?

We must make the desires of the King the great priority in our life. In over thirty-seven years of full-time ministry, I can say without hesitation that the Christian life is about Him, not us. It is following our King and His Kingdom rather than accepting Him into our busy lives.

Your mandate is to penetrate a corrupt kingdom and replace it with a glorious, loving, and eternal Kingdom. You were born to love from a pure heart and rule in humility. You *must* rise to your calling as His Warrior Bride. The hosts of heaven and hell are watching you with anticipation. This is the way of His unshakable Kingdom. There is no better way.

NOTES

1. John Wesley, *Daily Christian Quote*, http://dailychristianquote.com/dcq-suffer.html (accessed 1/7/10).

2. Os Guinness, *Prophetic Untimeliness* (Grand Rapids, MI: Baker Books, 2003), 86, 89, 91–93. Used by author's permission.

3. NT:2906 kraugh/ **krauge** (krow-gay'); from NT:2896; an outcry (in notification, tumult or grief):

(Biblesoft's New Exhaustive Strong's Numbers and Concordance with Expanded Greek-Hebrew Dictionary. Copyright © 1994, 2003, 2006 Biblesoft, Inc. and International Bible Translators, Inc.)

Chapter Notes

FOR MORE INFORMATION

Steve Harrison

c/o Bethany Urban Development

P.O. Box 8940

Minneapolis, MN 55408

Phone: 612-598-3270

http://www.loveontheedge.org

contact@loveontheedge.org

ALSO BY STEVE HARRISON

Book One, *Consuming Love* and Book Two, *Liberating Love*
of the three-book Warrior Bride Series

Available today from Ardor Media

Ardor Media is a division of Bethany Urban Development, a ministry
dedicated to transforming hearts, homes, and communities through a
prayer and worship lifestyle.

Ardor Media

P.O. Box 8940

Minneapolis, MN 55408 info@ardormedia.com

http://www.ardormedia.com